KALEIDOSCOPE
WARWICKSHIRE

Edited by Dave Thomas

First published in Great Britain in 1999 by
POETRY NOW YOUNG WRITERS
Remus House,
Coltsfoot Drive,
Woodston,
Peterborough,
PE2 9JX
Telephone (01733) 890066

All Rights Reserved

Copyright Contributors 1998

HB ISBN 0 75430 449 3
SB ISBN 0 75430 450 7

Foreword

This year, the Poetry Now Young Writers' Kaleidoscope competition proudly presents the best poetic contributions from over 32,000 up-and-coming writers nationwide.

Successful in continuing our aim of promoting writing and creativity in children, each regional anthology display the inventive and original writing talents of 11-18 year old poets. Imaginative, thoughtful, often humorous, *Kaleidoscope Warwickshire* provides a captivating insight into the issues and opinions important to today's young generation.

The task of editing inevitably proved challenging, but was nevertheless enjoyable thanks to the quality of entries received. The thought, effort and hard work put into each poem impressed and inspired us all. We hope you are as pleased as we are with the final result and that you continue to enjoy *Kaleidoscope Warwickshire* for years to come.

Contents

Alcester Grammar School
    Lucy Morris — 1

Alderman Smith School
    Victoria Jenkins — 2
    Charlotte Lyons — 2
    Emma Thompson — 3

Ash Green School
    Hayleigh White — 4
    Jenny Parsons — 4
    Hayley Owen — 5
    Helen Carey — 5
    Tasha Bishop — 6
    Alison Ford — 6
    Zak Moffat — 7
    George Reynolds — 7
    Craig Jefferson — 8
    Anthony John Barnes — 8
    Amy Cotton — 9
    Anthony Graham — 10
    Ashley Smart — 10
    Natalie Roberts — 11
    Emma Sugrue — 11
    Danielle Eddy — 11
    Rachel Durden — 12
    Claire Neale — 12
    Samantha Kirkham — 13
    Daniel Ryman — 13
    Nicole Dudley — 14
    Emma Eddy — 14
    Stacey Heslop — 15
    Nathan Hodgson — 15
    Paul Griffin — 16
    Faye Huxford — 16
    Jervinder Flora — 17

Emma Short	17
Liam Walsh	17
Danielle Smith	18
Kate Taylor	18
Germaine R Foster	19
Katherine Sands	19
Nikki Austin	20
Michelle Berry	21
Zoe Jewitt	22
Mahbir Pal Singh Thukral	22
Sophie Boulstridge	23

Avon Valley School

Ashleigh Culver	23
Joel Smith	24
Carly McIntyre	24
Sally Devine	25
William Biddle	25
Jason Davies	26
Krishna Calvert	26
Christopher Wakeleigh-Jones	27
Faye Davies-Lowde	27
Maria Walton & Emma Williams	28
Paul Doney	28
Matthew Baker	29
Anthony Lodge	30
Iain Wood	30
Andrea Howe	31
Andrew Williams	31
Martin Goodman	32
Kerrie Wood	32
Sacha Worton	33
Kayleigh Thomas	33
Daniel Dwelly	34
Frankie Hudson	34
Tina Phillips	35
Emily Young	36
Kane Potter	36

	Charmaine Eccles	36
	Nathan Parry-Hall	37
	Shaun Howells	37
	Craig Phillips	38
	Steven James	38

Ernesford Grange School
    Emma Smith   39

George Eliot School

	Charlotte Courtney	40
	Jemma Hyde	40
	Elizabeth Hyde	41
	Karl Nesbitt	42
	Thomas Smith-Phelps	43
	Chloe Ayres	44
	Stephanie Davidson	44
	Jo McDonald	45
	Dominique Cawthorne	46
	Graham Howard	46
	Melissa Balding	47
	Jill Barber	47
	Kevin Riley	48
	Thomas Caul	48
	Christopher Eeles	49
	Stuart Frisby	50
	Rubina Khan	50
	Laura Morris	51
	James Grant	52
	Dale Smith	52
	Catherine Bunn	53
	Simon Brooks	54
	Cherene Jade Chan	54
	Scott Glover	55
	Jonathan Boissonade	56
	Tammy Leigh	56
	Lara Chamberlain	57
	Julie Visgandis	58

	Laura Barnett	58
	Stacey Lenaghan	59
	Leanne Styles	60
	Rebecca Blower	60
	Lee Russell	61
	Amanda Douglas	61
	Faith L Fletcher	62
	Steven Davenport	63
Hartshill School		
	Carmen Silk-Neilsen	63
	Shyam Vithlani	64
	Lindsey Barnes	64
	Natasha Perkins	65
	Martin Hartshorn	65
	Colin Mullins	66
	Trisha Stallard	66
	David Yates	67
	Shani Coulton	67
	Laura Kent	68
	Emma McIver	68
	Laura Ashby	69
	Clare Taylor	70
	Jennifer Towers	70
	Laura McAdam	71
	Heather Yates	71
	Anna Hyams	72
	Graham Collins	72
	David Bates	73
	Natalie Gilder	73
	Lindsay Tynan	74
	David Monteith	74
	Kay Percival	75
	Matthew Glover	75
	James Wilson	76
	Aimeé Oakley	76
	Sarah King	77
	Natalie Osadciw	78

Nick Turner	78
Mark Reason	79
Paula Piff	80
Chris Skyner	80
Gayle Johnson	81
Kirsty Yates	82
David Miles	82
Louise Brown	83
Christine Yeomans	84
Laura Skyner	85
Jamie Barr	85
Emma Louise Bennett	86
Darren Brooks	86
Danielle Jack	87
Sam Swami	87
Melissa Day	87
James Rathbone	88
Jenny Rowson	88
Emma Ashby	89
Jemma Dunnachie	89
Matthew Brown	90
Helen Holt	90
Rebecca Ashby	91
Lorna Tarplin	92
Alan Lapworth	92
Sam Hands	93
Emma Spittle	94
Carly Slane	94
Michael Lapworth	95
Amy Matts	95
Kate Brown	96
Joanne Harborne	96
James Power	97
Ryan Miller	97
Emily Whopples	98
Gary Hughes	98
Lee Trembeth	98
Leigh Stallard	99

	Nicola Hadley	100
	Charlotte Brindley	101
	Cheryl Fox	101
	Hayley Jones	102
	Ryan Ashby	102
Henley High School		
	Chris Sharp	102
	Carrie Laity	103
	Katie Herrick	104
	Chris Freeman	105
	Lucy Swift	106
	Laura Compton	107
	Lucie Wheatcroft	108
	Rebecca Laing	109
	Hannah Smalley	109
	Joanna Hardman	110
	Robert Stone	111
	Alistair Barrett	112
Kenilworth School		
	Ruth MacDonald	113
	Luke Stanley	114
	Emma Ballard	114
	Natalie Johnson	115
	Elizabeth Harwood	116
	Laura McKay	117
North Leamington School		
	Philip Wiggins	117
	Rebecca Wallace	118
	Rebecca Robbins	118
	Fiona Moore	119
	Nisha Rai	119
	James White	119
	Zoe Millington	120
	Richard Evans	120
	Matthew Lester	120

Thomas Barnwell		121
Emily Holloway		122
Beth Mountford		122
Rachel Stickley		123
Joanne Burton		123
Christine Mathers		124
Kirsty Mansfield		125
Lisa Whittleton		126
Emma Thompson		126
Lucy Griffin		127
Rebekah Pink		127
Jackie Perry		128
Matthew Harris		128
Harriet Whitehead		129
Sasha-Marie Chapman		129

Rugby High School

Lizzie Beresford	129
Victoria Yeats	130
Angharad Rees-Jones	130
Jenna Curtis	131
Vikki Stone	132
Amina Malik	132
Itohan Ugiagbe	133
Lucy Pogson	134
Emily Reid	135
Emma Jeffs	136
Jasdeep Toor	136
Rebekah Greenslade	137
Suzanne Gilkes	138
Lisa Dale	138
Sahra Ali	139
Louise Leighton	140
Gela Veshagh	140
Juliette Harrisson	141
Joanne Konkel	142
Irene White	142
Cara Bemrose	143

Charlotte Parkins	144
Lynsey Smith	144
Claire Gladwin	145
Kate Dunlop	146
Ria Smulovic	146
Claire Gulliver	147
Natalie Hoath	148
Hannah Griffiths	148
Lucy Ogburn	149
Kirsty Lewis	149
Emma Alsop	150
Hannah Davies	150
Holly Inman	151
Meriel Close	152
Sarah Hughes	153
Charlie Winn	154
Amelia Lee	155
Lucy Keay	156
Alicia Mistry	156
Jasmine Reynolds	157
Tania Hayes	158
Sarah Peck	159
Rebecca Kelly	159
Lexy Lay	160
Miriam Sturdee	161
Margaret Bennett	162
Katy Cross	162
Debbie Holmes	163
Samantha Butterworth	164
Hannah Edwards	165
Hayley Eames	166
Emily-Jane Arbon	167
Jennifer Deeley	168
Sara Balsom	168
Emilie Day	169
Shelley Holland	170
Isabelle Jeffery	170
Lucy Faulkner	171

Amy Grewcock	172
Sarah Glenn	172
Hannah Bayliss	173
Stephanie Greer	174
Joanne Prior	175

St Benedict's RC High School

Daniel Bishop	175
Kathy McGreal	176
David Ryan	176
Matthew Torjussen	177
Andrew Roberts	177
Georgie Bradley	178
Jennifer Spires	178
Joanne Clarke	179
Genevieve Hughes	179
Nicola Torrance	180
Sara Andrews	180
Christopher Whittingham	181
Christopher Davies	181
Anna Middleton	182

Southam School

Laura Kerr	182
Sophie Palmizi	183
Oliver Longden	183
Hayley Leahy	184
Vicky Moore	184
Sarah Brooks	185
Gail Russell	185
Amy McTaggart	186
Wayne Clea	186
Alex Biggerstaff	187
Lisa Cooper	187
Jamie Maher	188
Rebecca McGovern	188
Becky Busby	189
Gemma Jackson	189

Leaona Bourton	190
Natalie Waters	190
William Bostock	191
Carol Hulme	191
Katie Webb	192
Lisa Scott	192
Dan Moreby	192
Stephen Smith	193
Natalie Baillie	193
Simon Hughes	194
Philippa Surgey	195
Adam Eastbury	195
Alex Elliott	196
Kayleigh Myczko	196
Wendy Dowdeswell	197
Sophie Eadon	198
Mark Anderson	199
Ginnene Taylor	200
Louise Owen	200
David Mugleston	201
Adam Robinson	201
Andrew Moore	202
Ceri Amphlett	202
Kirsty Anderson	203
Angela Cox	204
Claire Haughton	205
Anne-Marie Cosgriff	206
Lee Jones	206
Sally-Anne Southam	207
Alice Telford	207
Lynsey Worrall	208
Alice Wright	208
Charlie Hacker	209
Danny Brookes	210
Scott Simpson	210
David James Camps	210
Dawn Rawlings	211
Jenna Mahoney	211

Vicky Milburn	212
Hope Emily Jezzard	212
Michael McTaggart	213
Michelle Wallwin	214

Stratford High School

Tom Blizzard	214
Tomas Matthews	215
Claire Davies	215
Kimberley Powell	215
Jamie Southam	216
Gemma Simpson	216
Emily Podbielski	217
Andrew Briffett	217
Sarah Arnold	218
James Fernandes	218
Mark Roberts	219
Alexander Barons	219
Lydia Burton	220
Helen Goodman	220
Amy Bishton	221
Zoë Gibbons	221
Stewart Crow	222
Jack Wharton	222
Nicole Wein	223
Thomas Baker	224
Emma Jones	224
Melantha Thomson	225
Jennie Needham	225
Hannah York	226
Anna Sanders	226
Hannah Eastgate	227
Michelle De-la-Mare	227
Gemma Honor	228
Shelley Faulkner	228
David Rees	229
Ben Whybrow	229
Katie Shelton-Smith	230

Hayley Ash	230
Lisa Griffiths	231
Joy Middleton	231
Ella Selwood	231
Sally Hall	232
Tom Fidler	232
Claire Hawkins	233
Anthony Green	233
Amy Wein	234
Lucy Stanley	234
Hazel Ingram	235
Alexandra Sophie Delin	235
Sophie Parslow	236
Amanda Keech	236
Sophie Ellis	237
Lisa Leongamornlert	237
Selina Mayo	238
Craig Hodgkins	238
Katie Wood	239
Adrian Mitchell	239
Holly Perry	239
Kevin Holt	240
Siân Walters	240
Sarah Hicks	241
Elizabeth Blewer	241
Amiee Cotterill	242
Rachael Coombes	242
Claire May	243
Tom Cox	243

The Poems

THE JUNGLE

For Christmas I had a lovely new book
I couldn't resist it I had to take a look.
I opened the book and the next thing I knew
there stood an elephant and a monkey too.
I went to run but then I heard a gentle whisper
'Don't be scared.'

My knees were knocking, I began to shake
as down a tree slithered a snake.
I turned around to make an escape
but there in front of me stood a hairy ape.
'Hey little girl, don't run away.
All I want to do is have fun and play.'

We played hide and seek until it got dark.
Then all I heard was a familiar bark.
It was my dog Spike waking me up!

Lucy Morris (11)
Alcester Grammar School

It's The Last One Left

In our local Museum
We have a rare exhibit.
It's kept in a glass tank
It's the last one left.

In our local Museum
Lots of people come to see.
It has everything cared for
It's the last one left.

In our local Museum
Scientists stare at it.
It's so odd to look at.
It's the last one left.

In our local Museum
Kept in a glass tank.
Is a tree
It has to be looked after
It's the last one left.

Victoria Jenkins (14)
Alderman Smith School

Environment

Children in the playground
litter everywhere.
One cuts their hand
others get a scare.

Old lady walking down the road
dog mess on the floor.
One step forward
Crash! Bang! As she falls.

Toddlers by the sea
parent at their side.
Hand goes in, gets very wet
wasn't that near the sewage pipe?

People go round every day
leaving rubbish to decay.
But if I could have my way
The environment would be safe to play.

Charlotte Lyons (13)
Alderman Smith School

THE ENVIRONMENT!

Our environment
should be friendly and clean.
But everywhere you look
only rubbish can be seen
from cars, buses and lorries.
Oh, the fumes you can smell!
pollution in the air.
So who can we tell?
People should be warned
about the damage it's caused.
We should all stop and think
and just take a pause.
The countryside is wrecked
it's such a shame.
But all said and done
it's people who are to blame.
So, in the future,
people like me and you
should keep the environment healthy
because we all live in it too!

Emma Thompson (14)
Alderman Smith School

HALLOWE'EN

Hallowe'en, Hallowe'en.
Costumes look all horrible and mean.
Pumpkins with weird expressions
my mates are doing witch impressions.

Spooks and spirits are all about
scaring people no doubt.
Lurking here, lurking there
looking for a great scare!

All I hear is 'Trick or treat!
Give me something good to eat.'
Hallowe'en is time for fun
for spooks to play until the
rise of the sun.

Hayleigh White (12)
Ash Green School

SAD AND HAPPY

S ometimes I am sad
A nd angry with myself
D ad always tells me off if I am sad.

A nyway it is anger I don't understand
N or do my friends
D on't mess with anger it's not so nice.

H appy
A word that describes me
P eople often say, 'What are you happy for?'
P eople would say, 'She's in a funny mood today!'
Y ou should always be happy in whatever you do.

Jenny Parsons (14)
Ash Green School

THE SECRETS OF HALLOWE'EN

The creaky wooden stairs give me the shivers.
An old rocking chair rocks in the howling wind.
The children scream *Boo* in the dark lonely lanes.
Frightening people as they walk back to their candlelit homes.

Pumpkins with twisted, screaming expressions.
Crying out to monsters who come out only at the dead of night.
Spiders and mice crawling on the wooden attic floorboards.
Making tipping, tapping noises and crawling towards you.

Ghouls and ghosts mumble, their wails incoherent.
Zombies stagger towards you with outstretched arms.
Witches cackle whilst zooming through the sky.
Stroking their black cats with eyes so dark, yet so bright.

Hayley Owen (12)
Ash Green School

MY BALLAD

I hate sad days
they make me feel like I want to curl up
in despair
just for two hours or maybe all day.

I know I will have some happy days
but sometimes they seem
the same as the sad days.

I wish there was something I could do
which would make me feel ten times better.

And if there was I would do it all
of the time.

Helen Carey (14)
Ash Green School

PANTOMIMES

When I saw Cinders one day
she was running far away.

She was running on her own
I said 'Hello!' and she just groaned.

Cinders was running until she fell
she thought she'd ended up in hell.

She got up to find she'd lost her slipper
then she thought that she saw flipper.

She carried on running until she finds
a little cottage which was behind.

Cinders stayed there for a while
until she found a phone to dial.

A handsome prince who kindly said
'Will you come with me and wed?'

Tasha Bishop (12)
Ash Green School

SPOOOKS

H ere witches meet
A lways - it's never a treat
L ights all around you
L ots of horrible goo
O h watch mum's carpet
W ow look at that market!
E njoy yourself - have a good time
E ach of you are covered in grime.
N o one's allowed behind this line.

Alison Ford (11)
Ash Green School

WEIRD CHILD

I don't like egg
I've got a sore leg
so I went to bed with a very sore head.

I don't like bread
I banged my head.
My mum said
'What's all the banging?'

I shouted to my mum
I fell on my bum
so why don't you come and help me?

My mum came up
with my little brown pup
and gave me a cup of water.

She went back down
with a confusing frown.
She told my dad
that his son is sad.

Zak Moffat (14)
Ash Green School

BONFIRE

B is for bangers
O is for orange flickering flames
N is for the approaching night we love so much.
F is for falling rockets from the sky
I is for indigo rockets in the sky
R is for rivers of people coming through the gates
E is for the excitement all of the people are having.

George Reynolds (12)
Ash Green School

STUFF!

Toilet rolls, kitchen rolls
sausage rolls, bread rolls.
Big rolls, small rolls
large rolls, little rolls
Arctic rolls, chocolate rolls.
Swiss rolls, jam rolls
spring rolls, fig rolls,
fat rolls, thins rolls.

Apple pie, rhubarb pie
custard pie, chocolate pie,
meat pie, ham and egg pie.
Vegetable pie, steak and kidney pie
chicken and mushroom pie, mince and potato pie
fat pie, thin pie.

Donkey, monkey
house key, car key.
Shed key, bike key
fat key, thin key,
large key, little key.

This is all the *stuff* I like.

Craig Jefferson (14)
Ash Green School

THE BLUE WHALE

The blue whale swims
gracefully through the
deep blue seas looking
for forbidden food.

The peaceful creature
glides through the misty
water avoiding humans
looking after their young.

Anthony John Barnes (12)
Ash Green School

THE HAUNTED HOUSE

Late at night the boy was lost.
He'd left his mates but at what cost?
He saw a house went through the gate
Should he turn back before it's too late.
Knocked on the door, wondered if he should
It was then he saw the blood.
The door opened the boy peered in
He saw an old man with a sickly grin
'Come in young man.' the old man said.
Hairs stood up on the little boys head.
He beckoned him in with a craggy finger.
The boy knew there was no time to linger.
Off he ran into the dead of night.
Boy oh boy! Did he get a fright!
The old man chased him round and round
Far too late he saw the hound.
Big teeth bared, he barked and wailed.
The little boy knew he was nailed.
Eaten by the dog or caught by the man
Now was the time to hatch his plan.
Wake up quickly, do not scream
Be thankful it's only a dream!

Amy Cotton (14)
Ash Green School

PLAY THE GAME . . .

Life's a game
You risk the game known as your life.
You take chances at every turn.
After a mistake you learn not to do it again.
If you stroll through it, you won't take any chances.
The game will end on its own.
Someone else can end it without provocation.
Someone else can end it with your consent.
The biggest mistake is to end it yourself.

Anthony Graham (14)
Ash Green School

A GREAT ANTIQUE

Clitter
clatter
clop.
Horses make a lot.

Chant
rant
scream.
Fans make all of these.

Have a guess what it's about?
If you haven't! Scream and shout.
This thing is very unique
It's music itself - a great antique.

Ashley Smart (12)
Ash Green School

RAINBOW

R ed, yellow, blue and green
A mong other colours they can be seen
I f there's a storm or if it's raining
N ever mind, stop complaining
B ecause after the damp and misty weather
O h don't worry! It will get better
W hen the rainbow appears.

Natalie Roberts (12)
Ash Green School

TITANIC

Titanic was the greatest ship.
It glided through the sea.
Then it hit an iceberg and went down.
People were screaming and people were crying.
First class people were sure to survive.
Third class people were sure to die.
That was the end of the great Titanic.

Emma Sugrue (13)
Ash Green School

BONFIRE NIGHT

Bonfire Night stars in sight,
The colours on the bonfire are so bright.

The greatest thing about Bonfire Night,
Is the fireworks *whooshing* in the night.

With a nice warm fire to warm your fingers and toes,
Nobody knows how hot the fire glows.

Danielle Eddy (11)
Ash Green School

LIFE

A poem about life - a ball of fun
excitement and laughter see us run
into the sea up and down hills
over the fence and in the garden.
I love life with family and friends
all together that's how we spend our days.
If you could see me now you would see
how much I care.
When my mum does festivals she lets me bake the pies
and when it's all finished I help her do the sides.
My dad always helps me and I help with his woodwork
he lets me read my book while he goes with my sister
and feeds the ducks.
Life is something we're all lucky to have
and if you don't treat it right you'll go to hell.
It's time you won't get another chance
so take this chance in mind.

Rachel Durden (12)
Ash Green School

LOVE

Love, love is in the air.
Love, love is everywhere.
Your heart may be broken
but don't be mistaken
'cause love, love is in the air
and love, love is everywhere.

Claire Neale (14)
Ash Green School

DRAGONS

Dragons, fierce and scary.
Dragons, green and scaly.
Dragons pointed tails
Dragons breathe red-hot fire.

Some are fierce, but some are friendly.
The friendly dragons are the best
they are better than the rest.
Friendly dragons talk to you.
Fierce dragons blow fire at you.

Dragons are big dark ugly creatures
with sharp pointed tails.
Dragons green, big scary, red eyes.

Samantha Kirkham (12)
Ash Green School

A DUCK WITH A LITTLE LUCK

A duck a duck with a little luck
is taken to a little pond.
It's gifted with its beauty
very soft and furry.
Golden eyes shine at night
you throw some bread
it pecks the bread with its golden beak.

A duck a duck that's very hooked
is taken to a better place.
Golden flowers
little towers.
All the flowers smell as sweet as a rose
this place is what I would describe as heaven.

Daniel Ryman (12)
Ash Green School

START OF MY LIFE

Seventh of April 1984
just as my mum was shutting the door.
To go for a daily shop
I decided to come out with a pop.

Off to the hospital
in a mad rush.
I hope I'm not born in a bush.

Got there in time
I was just fine
and I was born about 11.35 pm.

Mum was in pain
Grandad brought me a train
He really couldn't get over I was a girl.

Mum and Dad took me home
now they will never be alone
and that was the start of my life.

Nicole Dudley (14)
Ash Green School

DEATH OF MY BIRD

As I walk down the stairs,
Looking for the bird in his cage.
'He's not there,' I thought.
Then I look on the floor of the cage,
I thought, 'He's dead.'
He looked like he was sleeping,
His light blue feathers had not moved.
My poor old bird named Joey was dead.

Emma Eddy (14)
Ash Green School

NIGHT

Night is when teenagers go clubbing,
It's when the stars and the moon come out.

Everybody goes to bed,
Everybody *knock, knock* on their head.

Night is quiet,
It's quite light when the stars shine above.

The moon above smiles at you
As you look out of your window at the night.

Animals come out at night and hunt
When no one can see them.

So don't be scared,
It's only the night!

Stacey Heslop (12)
Ash Green School

MONSTER

I'm *big*
I'm *hairy*
I may be *scary*!
But that's the way I am
If that's a *problem*
I'll *crush* you.
Like a tin can
Because
That's the way I *am!*

Nathan Hodgson (12)
Ash Green School

Fishing

Fishing is cool
when you go to the pool.
Bite alarms beeping
rods bending
reels squealing.
Who said fishing was peaceful
fish breaking the surface
sending circular ripples around the pond.
Beep another bite alarm
hold on it's mine!
I strike
Yes, my rod bends double.
I play the fish for 2 minutes
then I pull him over the rim of my landing net.
3lb at least.
What a fish!
A mirror carp!

Paul Griffin (13)
Ash Green School

The Moon

The moon is shining down on the silver landscape.
She is sad and lonely staring down below her.
She heaves a sigh which sends the leaves swirling
off the trees and on to the hard autumn ground below.
She is all alone!

It's time for her to leave now
and let the sun take her place.
She slips back into space where she
awaits her turn to go to earth again.

Faye Huxford (12)
Ash Green School

HALLOWE'EN

Hallowe'en, Hallowe'en is a sight.
Hallowe'en, Hallowe'en is a fright.
Children come to eat some candy
and one of their names was Andy.
You should see the adults' eyes
when children give them a fright.
So Hallowe'en, Hallowe'en is a fright
and guess what?
It's in the middle of the night.

Jervinder Flora (11)
Ash Green School

LIFE

Death will come to everyone one day
it will come to you.
Even when you least expect it
or even when you do.
So think about it - take my advice
and live life to the full.
So think about it one more time
and live life like you should.

Emma Short (12)
Ash Green School

COLOURS

Red means danger and yellow means the light,
Green is the grass below us and black is the night.
Purple is the happiness and blue means the sky,
Brown is the gloomy days and pink is you and I.

Liam Walsh (11)
Ash Green School

THE CHILD

What colour is the child inside?
The father is black.
The mother is white.
What colour is the child above
The answer is simple
The answer is love.
Tell me what you see when you look hard
into a child's heart.
Can you see a child with a nice heart?
But with somewhere deep down in it
there's sorrow.
So what do you think the answer is?
The answer is simple
the answer is love.

Danielle Smith (13)
Ash Green School

STARS

Stars are shining in the night sky.
When I see a shooting star
I make a wish.

The stars are so bright
in the day there's a sun
and at night there's a moon.

All the stars come out
to play but in the day
they go
away.

Kate Taylor (12)
Ash Green School

BONFIRE NIGHT

Logs alight,
Puffs of smoke,
Filthy and black,
It makes you choke.

Pink, yellow, red and green,
In the dark sky,
Bright lights can be seen.

Face glowing but hands so cold,
Instructions of safety you must be told.

Lots of noise,
Crackles and bangs,
Sound of rockets
Squeaks and clangs.

Germaine R Foster (14)
Ash Green School

FIREWORKS

F ifth of November
I s such a sight
R iver of bangs in the sky
E ating your favourite food
W ith pickles and cheese
O nions none for me, but some for you
R ivers of people at the door
K ids at the party, called *Bonfire Night*
S hame - another whole year to wait!

Katherine Sands (11)
Ash Green School

When I'm With You

When I'm with you I feel beautiful
I feel like there is Heaven around us.
When I look into your eyes I feel warm.
Everything in my body is racing and rushing,
Heart pounding, head ready to explode.
I dream of waves crashing against the rocks.
We are on top of the rocks making love.

With the sun's golden light beaming down on us.
The sweet smell of your hair just takes me away.
We begin to rise into the golden light.
I feel in ecstasy with your arms wrapped round me.
Then we begin to fade into the clouds,
We really are on a high.

You touch my face softly from my left eye to my chin.
You kiss me softly on my left ear.
And whisper if I did not know better I'd say you were an angel.
But in my eyes you're a God.

I begin to awake. I look up and you have vanished.
Who was he? I don't know!
Was he an angel come to show me the way?
There was a rose on my pillow.
A note with the words.
For you are my God and I will always look up to you.
I feel for you more than love
Amen Lord.

Nikki Austin (14)
Ash Green School

NAN

You lived your life until the very end.
From the day you were born, until the day you went,
You touched our lives,
You touched our hearts
Your never ending love never stopped.

Came a day, when you got so ill,
You forgot our names and mine too.
That sure did hurt me, my family too,
But I knew deep down inside, that you still loved us.
I looked into your eyes and you looked into mine,
A sort of smile came across your lips.
The first I had seen in quite a while,
I knew right then, I would never forget this moment, not ever.

Came the moment you drew your last breath.
You had fought so hard, it was time for you to rest.
God took you away, on your dying day,
You were suffering in pain, so He couldn't let you stay.
You died in glory and dignity,
With the love of everyone who knew you.

Now I stand and place a flower at your final resting place,
I draw a tear, I heave a sigh.
The memories we have made, the love that we share
Our special moments I will never forget
The more I thought, the more I knew, you did not die
You live on in our hearts and thoughts.

There is one last thing I should say
'I love you Nan, and I always have.'
I've said it once and I'll say it again,
'I love you Nan, and I always will.'

Michelle Berry (14)
Ash Green School

THE FRIGHT OUTSIDE MY BEDROOM TONIGHT!

There's a haunting feeling around tonight,
Howling, screaming you're in for a fright.
White ghouls flying in the air,
Argh! Somebody's already had a scare!

The monsters are lurking around already,
Staggering, not at all steady,
Skeletons talking, incomplete,
Incomplete,
And their soul is wrapped in a white sheet!

It's all over soon
When it died down, the full moon!

Zoe Jewitt (12)
Ash Green School

A KID'S LIFE

A kid's life is never easy
And the kids always feel queasy.
The school dinners stink,
They make the kids eyes blink.
I want the school to be a bombshell,
Before the teacher rings that bell.
The school uniform has had it,
And I love that PE kit.
I like my best friend,
But he is a bit around the bend.

Mahbir Pal Singh Thukral (12)
Ash Green School

THE RAINBOW

Red for romantic roses.
Yellow for the glaring sunbeams.
Pink for the dusky evening sunset.
Green for the glistening grass on a dewy winter's morning.
Orange for half ripened tomatoes in the garden.
Purple for the heather growing wildly on the rugged moors.
Blue for the lake reflected by the sky.
The rain has gone, the sun shines through.
The beautiful rainbow brightens up the day.

Sophie Boulstridge (12)
Ash Green School

IT

I had it since childhood
Its best friend was me.
There are many times I look
Back and see it and me.

The perfect child's playmate
It was you see, because
It was always there
And understanding to me.

It was always there, it was for me
Until I grew up it was there for me,
Because when I grew up I forgot it
How to call it, how to make it come
I tried everything to make it come,
But just now I saw a child with it
I wanted it back but I knew I
                didn't need it anymore.

Ashleigh Culver (12)
Avon Valley School

FOOTBALL

Football, football,
It's a mystery to me
I mean, what's all this stuff
about the left wing and
the right wing?
Sounds to me like some sort of bird
with a goal at each end
and a line down the middle
and a couple of blokes
running around on its back!

Joel Smith (11)
Avon Valley School

CRASH GO THE WAVES

Crash, crash go the waves
against my lonely boat
my ears feel like icebergs
And my fingers feel like icicles.

Row, row, I think, oh
Why do I feel so cold?
My toes, my nose
Oh why are they so cold?

As lonely as I feel I can't
give up
All I feel is bitterness
as I row my boat.

Carly McIntyre (12)
Avon Valley School

Food! Food!

I love peanut butter,
So people say I'm a bit of a nutter,
I love chicken 'n' chips
And I love cheesy dips.

I love to drink Irn Bru,
But I hate my mother's stew,
I hate the smell, it's yuk!
It's in the saucepan, come and look!

I like to eat a bit of fish,
And it's my mum's favourite dish,
I love to eat big birthday cakes,
They're like the ones my mum makes.

Sally Devine (11)
Avon Valley School

Football Is My Life

Football is my name.
Football is my game.
Football is my life.
I'd rather have it than a wife.

Football is what I eat,
Football is what I wear on my feet.
Football is what I drink.
Football is what I think.

Football is what I called my pup,
When I picked up the winning cup.

William Biddle (11)
Avon Valley School

JINGLE BELLS

Jingle bells, jingle bells
Mum's overrun
Jingle bells, jingle bells
Christmas is fun
Jingle bells, jingle bells,
We're going shopping
Jingle bells, jingle bells
My mum is dropping.

Jingle bells, jingle bells
It's *Christmas Day!*
Jingle bells, jingle bells
It's Christmas, *hooray!*
Jingle bells, jingle bells
I play with my presents
All of the day.
Jingle bells, jingle bells
I hope next Christmas
Is not far away.

Jason Davies (12)
Avon Valley School

KITTENS

K   ittens cute and soft,
I   rresistible to touch,
T   o stroke, soft like cotton wool,
T   o touch, soft and cuddly,
E   ars small and silky,
N   aughty little creatures!
S   till, they're only babies.

Krishna Calvert (12)
Avon Valley School

FOOTBALL STARS

Although I'm feeling a bit unwell
I've sat and written a poem
About some famous football stars
Like Lee and Michael Owen.

By playing for their country
These men have made their name
For putting all their heart and soul
Into their football game.

With speed and skill out on the field
They always give their best
Inspiring others, just like me
To be better than the rest.

Christopher Wakeleigh-Jones (13)
Avon Valley School

SLIME

'Slime' . . . *ugh* . . . so gooey, so revolting
My brother had some from the shop.
It sits in his room in a pot,
It's green and it wobbles when it moves.

I swear it's alive, I'm positive.
'Oh no, he's home!' Sarah looked out of the window,
He was with his mates,
And they all had slime too.
'So I'm going to hide his slime.'

Faye Davies-Lowde (11)
Avon Valley School

TITANIC

Titanic, the unsinkable ship
set sail on its first and final trip

You are safe as can be down in the hold
it cannot happen, they were told

The fog was thick, the icy wind cold
it cannot happen, we were told

What's that in front, oh no, it's too late!
A crash a bang, this noise I hate

What's happening? I'm wet, I'm cold
it cannot happen, I was told

'Women and children' went out a cry
what will happen, will I die?

We were so many, lifeboats so few
no room for passengers, no room for the crew

I feel guilty now, I know my fate
for others sadly, it was too late!

Maria Walton & Emma Williams (13)
Avon Valley School

BMX-ING

Bmx-ing is the best
Mine is better than
all the rest
When I do a trick or jump
When I hit the ground
I make a thump.

When I catch a little fish
I put it in my little dish
I take it home for my tea
I put it in the oven for my
Wife and me.

Paul Doney (13)
Avon Valley School

FOOTBALL CRAZY!

He's football crazy,
He's football mad,
Football has taken away the little sense he had.

He starts running down the wing,
He shoots for the goal,
He spoons it at the ref,
Then he gets a red card,
He says 'Ref, give me a chance,'
The ref says 'Go away,'
Then he says 'I'm simply mad about football.'

He's football crazy,
He's football mad,
Football has taken away the little sense he had.

The ball goes off for a throw,
The captain says 'Come here,'
Then he says 'Take the throw,'
He asks then 'Why?'
'I let you take the throw 'cause
you're simply mad about football.'

Matthew Baker (12)
Avon Valley School

THE NIGHTMARE

It was seven o'clock at night
and there was a bang on the door.
'Who is it?' I shouted
No one answered.
I opened the door and
no one was there.
I heard someone
breathing heavily down
my neck like a draught
coming through a door.
I went downstairs to see
what was happening but
there was no one.
Then I shouted my dad's
name and he answered
whilst he was on the
settee with a bottle sat
in his lap.

Anthony Lodge (13)
Avon Valley School

THE WIND

When the wind whistles
The leaves fall to the ground
They fall so slow
They don't make a sound.

They crisp and curl
They wrinkle and crackle
Then the wind blows them away.

Iain Wood (13)
Avon Valley School

THE SEASIDE

The sea is blue
hot and cold.
People are all swimming
in the sea.

Donkeys walking
at the seaside.
Sand falling through
your fingers and toes.

Mothers, fathers, brothers and sisters
all enjoying themselves.
People bathing in the sea
sand all as golden as ever.
The seagulls all flying
up high in the blue sky.
The water all crashing on
the big brown rocks.

Andrea Howe (11)
Avon Valley School

THE STEAM TRAIN

The train goes flying down the track
I hear the wheels go clackety clank
As it zooms past I feel the wind blowing
my hair all over the place
It is now really picking up pace
I can see the train go into the distance,
But I can still smell the soot
Tomorrow I will watch from the
warmth of the railway man's hut.

Andrew Williams (12)
Avon Valley School

MY LITTLE BROTHER

My little brother is such a pain
he always gets his own way all the time
my little brother is so annoying
he bugs me every day.

My little brother gets away all the time
he never gets caught or told off
instead it's blamed on me, yes me
and it's really ticking me off!
My little brother I want
to wring his neck
if he does not stop
I'll end up a nervous wreck

My little brother
it makes me sad
but I think I can say
'You're driving me
mad!'

Martin Goodman (11)
Avon Valley School

A CANDLE

A bright white statue, with snow falling down,
looking like a moth's wing, as it forms its own sculptures.
The flame, like a dancing petal, sways in the wind.

The dark wick gives light as the flame stretches high.
The smell reminding you of a birthday cake,
when you extinguish the candles.
Smoke whirls, twirling, as you blow the candle out
And then it's dead!

Kerrie Wood (12)
Avon Valley School

DRAGON

Fly my winged reptile,
into my mind.
Lock your golden claws onto my wounded heart.
Your sapphire eyes, your silver scales,
your ruby heart glowing through the darkness.

Time shall not wait for you,
as you glide through the clouds,
your muscular wings a'beating.
Blow your flame to warm my hearth,
my eyes, my lips, my bones.
You are portrayed as a warlord,
savaging the Earth below,
But, come to me my majestic beast,
let your soul blaze the
sky!

Sacha Worton (12)
Avon Valley School

MY THOUGHTS

When I wake up I close my eyes
to see what I can see
I see lions, tigers, trees and seas
all things that mean a lot to me

I like to listen to my thoughts
about the lions, tigers, trees and seas
but when I open up my eyes
all I can see is my plain old room
and nothing means the same
to me.

Kayleigh Thomas (12)
Avon Valley School

MY FRIEND GARY

My friend Gary can do anything
He can jump out of a plane
Without a parachute or
Play in the mud and get dirty.
He can write with his tongue.

My friend Gary can do anything
He can kick the teacher and not be noticed
Or stroke a wild rabbit and it won't run away
And even stand in the middle of a road
And not be run over.

My friend Gary can do anything
He doesn't have homework
Or a mum or dad,
He doesn't ride a bike
Or anything like that.

Now you might be dying
To have a friend like this
Now you can have this friend whom
I like so much because he lives in your
Head and he's your imaginary *friend!*

Daniel Dwelly
Avon Valley School

ANIMALS

Animals can be big or small,
Animals can be short or tall,
Animals, animals everywhere,
They're even crawling under that chair,
Stop barking, you silly dog,
And stop chasing after that mouse
Mystic Mog.

Animals can be fast or slow,
Some like to tread on my toes,
Some animals can be lazy,
Some animals can be crazy.

Frankie Hudson (11)
Avon Valley School

MY TRUE LOVE IS

As deep as the ocean
My true love is
As sweet as candyfloss.
His brown hair gets tossed
in the wind.
He's so cuddly
and soft
like my teddy bear.
So cute,
My true love is
He is a fish
and I am twins,
We don't match very well.
He's sensitive
but also moody
My true love is.
He shares
And he loves animals.
He loves to be at home,
in his warm bed
with the comfort of big ted.
My true love is
The sweetest boy ever
And I love him!

Tina Phillips (14)
Avon Valley School

I LIKE...

I like the smell of fresh-cut grass on a sunny morning.
I like the sight of horses galloping in a field full of grass.
I like the taste of sweet strawberries crushing between my teeth.
I like the touch of rain falling between my fingers.
I like the sound of horses' hooves clacking on the ground.

Emily Young (11)
Avon Valley School

I LIKE

I like the smell of toast burning in the toaster.
I like the sight of cakes on the table.
I like the taste of fizzy sweets after lunch.
I like the feel of my bed at night.
I like the sound of football crowds running down the street.

Kane Potter (11)
Avon Valley School

TEACHERS

Teachers, teachers, everywhere
Teachers here, teachers there.
All day long they're in their rooms
Marking books and talking to you.
Everybody's in the room, looking at you, talking to you
Everybody's in the room working hard
Like they should.

Charmaine Eccles (13)
Avon Valley School

DARK DAYS OF THE WAR

It was the night that gave me a fright
The sound of gunfire with the light of the
bullets across the dark sky.
The sounds of people falling down dead in the trenches
People running and being shot down
Their bodies lie dead or injured on the ground.
People running by as the enemy gets closer and closer
but cannot get through the rusting barbed wire.
Shells hitting the ground, shaking the people
nearby falling down.
Dead bodies everywhere.
The rain pattering down on them,
The thunder roaring in the sky.
It's time to say goodbye to my friend
as he falls down dead.

Nathan Parry-Hall (13)
Avon Valley School

ROLLERBLADING

Rollerblading is the best
I am better than all the rest
When I do a trick or jump
I hit the ground, I make a
thump!
When I get back up
My knees are hurt.
I keep on trying till it
works.

Shaun Howells (13)
Avon Valley School

DARK NIGHTS

It was a cloudy night
I was walking down the street
I saw a clock tower
I saw a dark figure by the tower
I said 'Who is there?'
I said 'Who is there?' No reply.
Just as I turned away, the figure said 'Hello.'
I turned around and went to the tower.
No one was there so I turned around again.
I saw a shadow, but no body
It was not Hallowe'en and the clock had no light
That I knew of.

The clock struck midnight
Dong! Dong! Dong! Dong! Dong! Dong!

Craig Phillips (13)
Avon Valley School

THE SKY

When I look up to the sky
It always makes me cry.
When it starts to rain
It puts me in pain.
When it starts to snow
It gives me a blow.

When I see the sun
I want a hot cross bun.
I don't like the wind
'Cause I always want to sing.

Steven James (13)
Avon Valley School

Forever Friends

Forever friends - if only that were true,
I'm still quietly amazed by the change undergone by you.
You used to be a true friend - so generous and kind,
What possessed you to change? Are you out of your mind?
I met you six years ago - we were inseparable back then,
Now you're like a stranger - do you care? If so, when?
You're a shadow of yourself, it's like you've shed your old skin,
To me you're an enigma that's wearing my patience thin.
Now you've aligned yourself with new friends -
                                you pretend I don't exist.
Everything you do is done with an evil twist,
Throughout the good and bad times, true friends should always be there
To offer support and show that they care.
That was the case until not so long ago,
Then you decided I was not worthy enough to know.
At last your true colours have shone through,
You've helped me realise I don't need friends like you.
Your new attitude came out of the blue,
You treat people like something found on the bottom of your shoe.
I don't know what's filled you with such hatred and spite,
You're now quite content with picking unnecessary fights.
I quite happily accept that we're no longer friends,
But you could have at least tried to make amends.
I've nothing to apologise for - I've done nothing wrong,
Why don't you swallow your pride - or do you think you're too strong?
This shows that 'forever friends' can be an empty cliché,
Because friendship is not always permanent whereas
                                ignorance is here to stay.

Emma Smith (15)
Ernesford Grange School

DEATH OF A MOTHER

You're gone, now how am I to cope
Without your guidance?
Without your scope?
I don't know what to do,
Or where to turn.
My life has died
As your ashes burn.

Why now?
Why did you have to go?
I'm left in this cruel world,
All alone.
Wait for me up there in the clouds.
I'll meet you soon,
But not right now.
Life must go on
If not your own,
I'll always expect your presence
                          at home!

Charlotte Courtney (13)
George Eliot School

MY GRANDAD

I love him so dearly
I cherish him so much
I love his long brown curly hair
And his soft warm touch.

I hope and pray
Each day and night
His life will still remain
I hope that God's cruel hands
Do not take him away.

I do realise now it's not fair of me
To pray each night and day
For his life is almost over
But we love him all the same.

His days are spent with morphine
And his nights with endless pain
But my memories are forever
And his smile will never fade.

Jemma Hyde (13)
George Eliot School

HARE

Enemy magnet!
His eyes are like traffic lights,
They tell you when to *stop!*
'Don't go any further,' they say.
His ears are mountains,
   echoing in the shadows.
His pencil-mark fur,
   it writes darkness for him.
His horn-like tail pricks the
   innocent air as he bounces
   along the mossy ground.
This rare, wild animal,
He's a speeding car-killing sound.
His muscular legs,
   thumping like a baby's heart,
   as his foe approaches.
The bouncing ball moves back
   like a backward clock.
Just to escape in time,
   before the bomb explodes.

Elizabeth Hyde (12)
George Eliot School

THE CREEPY CASTLE

Bang!
Goes the big brown door
as it shuts.
Creeping around
the dark gloomy castle.
Squeak! Squeak! Squeak!
Go the floorboards
As I walk.
Whoosh!
Goes a bat
as it flies past me.
Going up the dark gloomy
stairs
I can see
spiders
and other insects.
They give me the shivers.
Squeak! Squeak! Squeak!
It must be a mouse
but
who's there, I wonder?
As I reach the top of the stairs
I see a door
open so I investigate.
I open the door then
I can see a
pers . . . Ahhhhh!

Karl Nesbitt (11)
George Eliot School

A Village Life!

Dairy-milk clouds surface on a vibrant blue sky,
The country fields were seeded to the brim.
A real country village!

A car would always go by, swelling up the prickly hedges.
It wasn't a modern car,
It was a Classic beauty.
The car would have no speckle of dust,
Only 3cms thick layer of polish,
It would glaze in the fiery sun.
There were a few old limestone cultured shops,
And a small petrol pump
To round up the cars on the way through the dense area.

At the end of the day,
The farmers would arise for a smooth frothy pint,
They would gallop a gulp and put back the pint,
A cream-layered moustache would appear.

Disguising mirages split marigold sunsets,
Crimson outbreaks shatter the sky into cracks,
If only every place reflected this!

Behaviour spread
Like a bouncy ball
Or butter being pulled vertical on a reflecting knife
And then is built ... this!

Thomas Smith-Phelps (13)
George Eliot School

SUNSET OF LOVE

I watch the sunset fading to nothing
Close my eyes but still I see
Spectacular arrays of dimming light
Slipping far away from me.

The bright moon appears out of the darkness.
A shining torch in the black.
Until it appears, sky has no feature,
It was what the dusk had lacked.

The silky sand slips between my fingers
And pours down onto the beach.
It comes and goes like waves lap to and fro,
But that's all we have to teach.

The sunset is gone and darkness bestows
I close my eyes and I sigh.
The sand has settled right beside my feet
I bow my head and I cry.

Chloe Ayres (13)
George Eliot School

TITANIC

The ship of dreams, sailing ahead,
With thousands of people aboard,
But what people don't know is that
An iceberg is slowly approaching,
While they're warmly tucked up in bed.

Titanic hits! Oh God, a big hole!
And the ship starts to fill up with water.
The passengers wake up and start to panic,
Before they go down with the sinking Titanic.

The panic, so many people trying to get to safety,
The chaos, the screaming of all the worried people,
The ship goes down,
And leaves people weak and feeble.

The people flap around like fish,
Trying to keep themselves warm.
Most people are dead, the ship is too late,
To live was most people's wish.

Stephanie Davidson (13)
George Eliot School

THE STRAY DOG

She was found wandering the streets,
Her fur was matted with old age dirt,
Her ribs were showing through her skin.

She had parasites, fleas and diseases,
She was frightened, timid and scared,
Her face was extremely pitiful.

I bathed her and brushed her fur out,
I cut out the knots and injected her,
Who could let her get into this state?

After her bath and her brush,
She was re-homed to a loving family,
She deserved what she got, her new life,
Who could have done such a thing?

I feel anger towards the owner,
I feel sad as well to know,
That this sort of thing happens,
Every single day.

Jo McDonald (11)
George Eliot School

My Grandad

He would lie there all day and night,
putting up a terrible fight.
He was put through hell
because of the pain.
It kept happening over and over again.
He would light up my life when a smile broke free,
He thought 'Why does this have to happen to me?'
I would pray every night, and hold on tight
That his life would not end tonight.
But it didn't work, as he closed his eyes
He was lifted through the sunny skies.
He was taken away, to a place far away,
He will never come back, he just couldn't stay.
I love him so much, he had such a warm touch,
I never got the chance to say 'Bye.'
But he was such a brilliant guy!

Dominique Cawthorne (13)
George Eliot School

The Gunshot

An explosion of sound cuts through my ears
The bullet pierces my breast.
The cold metal burns my heart
My vision blurs.
I fall, the killer discreetly escapes
The light fades.
I leave the world and head to the next
The pain reaches a climax.
My flesh is burning, my skin is cold
The burning has left me, the fire is out.
    I am dead!

Graham Howard (13)
George Eliot School

THE MONSTER DOWN THE MINE

The monster down the mine
Eats children at nine.
He puts them on the track
They never come back.

They go to sleep
They never peep
The monster roars
At half-past four.

The monster down the mine
Eats children at nine.
He puts them on the track
They never come back.

Melissa Balding (11)
George Eliot School

FLOWER IN THE BREEZE

An infinite curve,
Delicately twines
Around my stem in nerve,
Petals flow in time.

A delicate breeze,
Disturbing my mirage.
The stem bows on my knees,
Soaking, needing charge.

Meteorites landing,
Transparent crystals lie
Leaving my life standing,
I wither, don't need to die.

Jill Barber (13)
George Eliot School

THE TREE

The tree
Stands all alone, on a hill
Its branches forking outwards
Reaching to the sky for its life.

The tree
Birds come and land, perching on its arms,
And make their small house aloft.
As it sways in the wind, they chirp.

The tree
As the icy winds blow up, in and around
The leaves turn brown and fall
They drop, swinging from side to side, then crunch.

The tree
Solitude is all that it knows,
As it stands all alone, its soul aches
As the children play, laughing and shouting with joy.

The tree
It hears the chainsaw's roar
As it cuts into its side,
Now, nothing more than a table, a chair . . . or a door.

Kevin Riley (13)
George Eliot School

THE DEATH OF LOVE

An emptiness, no feeling
My heart gets worse, not healing.
Your voice I do not hear,
Your death I always fear.
With me you are not dealing
And you are nowhere near.

I have no need for love,
I have no peace, no dove,
All my heart is gone,
With love I'm finally done.
I hear things from above
I have no need for fun.

Thomas Caul (14)
George Eliot School

TWISTED

Why doesn't she want me?
I just don't see why.
Is it my ears or my eyes?
Is it down inside,
My voice, my walk or the way I talk?
If she does what shall I do?
If not, I'll have to move on.
Whatever the truth,
I must find out.
I don't wish to live alone.

Why does she want me?
I just don't see why.
Is it my ears or my eyes?
Is it down inside,
My voice, my walk or the way I talk?
If she does what shall I do?
If not, I can move on.
Whatever the truth,
I must find out.
I wish to live alone.

Christopher Eeles (14)
George Eliot School

LOVE, OF THE STRONGEST KIND

These feelings I'm bottling up inside,
Are taking over me.
I'm going to have to tell her soon,
Set my feelings free.
Why does it have to be so hard,
To open up my heart,
And if I could,
I never would,
Know just where to start.

Then sitting in the park that night
The love became too hard to fight
That moment I looked into her eyes
To see the starry, moonlit skies.
She bottled out,
And walked away,
My loved locked up for another day.

Stuart Frisby (13)
George Eliot School

I AM THE BEST

The writer of this poem
Is good at bowling
And always rolling
Faster than a bowling ball.

As small as Mr Jacks,
Always eating Black Jacks
As keen as can be
Right up to the knee.

As bright as the North Star,
As quick as a car,
As far as I know,
I'm the best, can't you see?

As wicked as I am,
And clever as I am
I'm bright as you can see,
So goodnight and sleep tight.

Rubina Khan (12)
George Eliot School

ANGEL

A guardian angel,
Watches over me.
Wherever I go,
Whatever I do,
She's always there,
Watching me.
Seeing that I never stray,
Making sure I always stay,
On the right path.

I know she's there,
Caring for me.
My hurts are healed,
My fate is sealed.
I'm never alone,
It's me,
And my guardian angel.

Laura Morris (14)
George Eliot School

MY DOG

I can't believe how many mistakes
My master makes,
He went off in the kitchen
And came back without my 'Shapes'.

I'm browned-off sitting waiting
I'll go in there alone,
So many goodies to choose from,
I think I'll have marrowbone.

Quite tasty and delicious
I've ate it and it is gone,
Selecting through my goodies
Oh, I'll have another one!

I know I'm putting weight on,
I'm cheating on my diet
But I'm eight and can't be bothered,
I'll sneak another on the quiet.

Oh, a tragedy's just happened,
I'm horrified to say
My master's just caught me,
And hid my goodies away!

James Grant (14)
George Eliot School

BLUE

Blue is the colour of
The deep blue sea,
Cool, calm serenity.
Blue is the colour of a mood,
But blue can also be rude!

Blue is the colour that best suits me,
Blond hair, blue eyes,
What else could it be!
On a sunny day, the sky is blue,
Everyone loves it - I bet you do.

Dale Smith (13)
George Eliot School

WAR

War is suffering and wrecks people's lives,
Departs husbands from children and wives.
Buildings destroyed and the land's a mess,
All the nature is getting less and less.

War is horrible and people get hurt,
Lots of bodies end up in the dirt.
Blood on your clothes and in your hair,
You've killed someone, but do you care?

Soldiers fight and just for money,
Risk their lives now that's not funny.
They wait for bombs day and night,
For their country they must fight.

War is horrible and people die,
Injured, disabled or they lose an eye.
Either way it's not very nice,
So before you fight please think twice.

Think of those who fight to their grave,
They fight in a war, does that make them brave?
When the war is over there's a sigh of relief,
But for a lot of people it's a time for grief.

Catherine Bunn (14)
George Eliot School

THE PARK

As I walk through the park at night,
I see the lights flickering,
The trees swaying in the wind.
As I look up at the moon,
I see a dot then loads more.
I remember they're stars
Then I look across.
There it is, the moon shining brightly.
As I walk home, I see the gates
All silver and beautiful.
Then on the ground,
A flower, different colours -
Red, purple, green and then in the middle, yellow,
Then ahhh a bee chasing me.

Simon Brooks (11)
George Eliot School

CHOCOLATE TREAT

There it is 50p
That's the one that's right for me.
Unpeel the gold and silver wrapper,
Hurry, hurry, faster, faster.
Tastes of dairy cream,
That feels like a dream.
I feel it disappearing,
Going down a slope.
It's about to drop,
It's not going to stop.
Going,
Going,
Gone!

Cherene Jade Chan (12)
George Eliot School

THE GLOVERS

Mrs Glover, going shopping,
Wasn't pleased and so she glared,
'Kiddies *please*' she said quite crossly,
'How can Mummy brush her hair?'

Off she went with her umbrella,
For it had begun to rain,
Said 'Now please be good you kiddies,
Till I get back home again.'

So she waited on the corner,
In the rain to catch the bus,
Kiddies waved and 'Well' said Scotty,
'Fancy saying that to us.'

Looking high, looking low,
They were making such a noise,
Throwing clean clothes everywhere,
Looking for their Christmas toys.

Scotty looked around the bed,
Kyle was pulling out the drawers,
'Nothing here' Scott shouted loudly,
Crawling round on all fours.

Running round all excited,
Didn't hear Mum come home,
When she saw such a mess,
'No! No!' she shouted
'That will make Daddy moan.'
Up to bed feeling really sad,
Now they know it's not so wise,
To make a mess and upset Daddy,
And almost ruin their Christmas surprise.

Scott Glover (11)
George Eliot School

Winter

The ducks disappear and geese too,
The wind howls and branches shake.
A rabbit burrows for a hole,
White flakes start to fall,
It is cold, very cold.

The snow is still falling,
It is a cold, beautiful morning.
The trees have been smothered in snow,
The ground is white and soft,
It is cold, very cold.

Children are playing in the snow,
Throwing snowballs, building snowmen.
Robin redbreast hops in the garden,
It is a beautiful, picturesque winter's day,
It is cold, very cold.

Jonathan Boissonade (11)
George Eliot School

Skinny Daddy-Long-Legs

Skinny daddy-long-legs
Umbrella feet.
Went to the pictures
Couldn't find a seat.
Finally found a seat
Fell fast asleep
Skinny daddy-long-legs
Fell through the
Seat.

Tammy Leigh (12)
George Eliot School

AEROPLANE

I'm going on an aeroplane, my family and me,
I'm wondering how high we'll go and just what we will see.
My stomach is a fluttering and I really need a drink,
Oh heck my legs are shaking it must be nerves, I think.

It's mega claustrophobic in a 757 jet,
It's like being in a sardine can, but I'm not panicking yet.
The seat belt sign comes on, I'm really in a tizzy,
The stewards and stewardesses do their little ditty.

We taxi down the runway waiting to depart,
The engines roar, everyone's quiet and I'm trying to act smart.
We wait a second then it's off with one almighty thrust
Oh yes I'm panicking now that's right, I've got to get this sussed.

We're taking off we're taking off, the ground goes by so fast
I'm forced in my seat too scared to move
How long will this feeling last?
We're up so high and over the sea there isn't much to do
Oh gosh what's that they're giving me, drinks and dinner too?

After dinner still up high I dare not look down
The plane starts tipping suddenly but we're only banking round.
I see the island there so small, that's where we're going to be
On that island for two whole weeks my family and me.

I'm going on an aeroplane, my family and me,
I'm wondering how high we'll go and just what will we see . . .

Lara Chamberlain (11)
George Eliot School

Take Me Away From Here

Take me away from here God,
Take me far away.
Take me away from here God,
I don't want to stay.

There's strangers all around me,
That don't seem to know or care,
There's strangers all around me,
That bully me everywhere.

Everywhere I go,
I feel lost and scared,
Everywhere I go,
I feel unprepared,

And every face I see,
Is the face of a bully,
Every face I see,
Is staring at me.

And what am I to do,
Only to ask you,
To take me away from here God,
Take me far away.
Take me away from here God,
I don't want to stay.

Julie Visgandis (11)
George Eliot School

Snow

Softly, softly falls the snow
From the heavenly sky,
Acting like the world's best show
But always the snow comes to die.

In the morning, where has it gone?
But I looked up, how the sun shone
Softly, softly falls the snow from
The heavenly sky
But always the snow comes to *die.*

Laura Barnett (11)
George Eliot School

FLAMING FIRE!

>The air is hot
>What is happening?
>Flames burst out
>High up in the sky
>Smoke fills the air
>Like a thick blanket!
>Woods catch fire,
>Flaming fire!

Flaming hot boots
As red and as hot as ever!
Kicking hot boots, beating fire
Flying through the air,
Flaming fire!

>Spreading fast
>Quick get out of the way
>Here they come,
>Red flaming fire.
>Wherever you are,
>*Stop, look, listen!*
>In the air smoke lies,
>Fire everywhere,
>Flaming fire!

Stacey Lenaghan (11)
George Eliot School

FIRE! FIRE!

Red-hot flames!
Burning all around me,
People screaming,
Flames burning hot,
The hotness getting closer,
But wait!

Hear sirens screaming,
The red and orange flames,
The trees falling,
Flames spreading,
Trapped!
No escape!
Water from the hoses
At last help on its way,
I think I'm saved!

Leanne Styles (11)
George Eliot School

FROSTY WINTER

It covers the grass like a soft white blanket,
Early in the morning you hear your feet go crunch on it.
It's so cold it melts in your hand,
It lies there like a frozen statue.
It's colder than wind, rain and snow,
You get a shiver down your body
Every time you touch it.
You have to wear warm clothes
To go out in it,
So what can it be?
The slippery slimy ice or the cold icy frost.

Rebecca Blower (11)
George Eliot School

THE LONG DISTANCE LORRY DRIVER

Sitting in my lorry, driving along
I turn on my radio and sing a song,
It's a lonely job all on my own
I've got miles to go before I go home.
The roads are all busy
It makes me go dizzy
With cars going this way and that.

At last I arrive at the port of St Ives
The end of a hard day's work
I get watered and fed, then get in my bed,
Now that my day is done.

Lee Russell (11)
George Eliot School

THE WORM

I am a worm
Creeping through the long thick grass,
Hoping to complete my journey.
There is a bird high in the sky,
I dig fast in the warm soft soil,
It is heading right for me like a dart,
Heading for a dartboard.
I dive into the soil,
The bird dives like an aeroplane out of control,
Its beak pinches my skin,
I struggle to get free like a mouse in a trap,
I wriggle frantically.
The bird drops me by mistake,
I have escaped,
I am so relieved!

Amanda Douglas (11)
George Eliot School

A Poem About Life

Life is a bundle of fun,
Life has its ups and downs.
Life can sometimes drown,
Life can be exciting.
Life can be enticing.
Life can be had, or
Life can be bad.
Life can be right or wrong,
Life will make you bite your tongue.
Life can be a shiver down your spine,
Life can be a lift up your line.
Life is a fantasy of love,
Life is second best to above.
Life can make you create a fist, or
Life can be a risk.
Life can be so bright, or
Life can be just a touch of sunlight.
Life can be a challenge or a dagger,
Life otherwise would be a stagger.
Life isn't easy,
Life wasn't meant to be easy-peasy.
Life may be hard,
Life doesn't mean you're barred.
Life can be joyful and jolly,
Life doesn't make you a dolly.
Life may be all over but you can never
Say it's all over and done.
Life's life and it's a bundle of fun.

Faith L Fletcher (14)
George Eliot School

THE WAR

The army marches to battle hoping they'll return,
They charge at the enemy with force and bravery,
The deafening sound of gunshots echo in the air,
Blood dripping from bodies staining on the ground,
Desperate cries from between dull lifeless corpses,
The battle continues, bodies being trampled,
Our army wins but what is the victory to the dead?

Steven Davenport (11)
George Eliot School

MY MONSTER

My monster is round and hairy,
He thinks he's fierce, and he thinks he's scary
His hair is green, it grows and grows,
His nails are yellow, and so are his toes,
His seven red eyes peer out of his head,
At night he sleeps underneath my bed,
His mouth is full of sharp white fangs,
He lumbers along with bumps and bangs.

My monster's got a runny nose,
And when it's dark the snot on it glows,
You'll hear him from a long way off,
You'll hear him shuffle, sneeze and cough,
His skin's all grey and spotty and tough,
His face is smooth, but his hands are rough,
His tummy is huge and hairy and round,
It's now so fat it nearly touches the ground.

So, my monster is round and hairy,
But underneath's really not very scary.

Carmen Silk-Neilsen (12)
Hartshill School

NIGHTMARES

A light bright face stares down
It sits on clouds which look like snow
The brightness went and it started to get
Darker and darker.
     Why?
Why did this have to happen?
I tried to wake myself, but it didn't work.
Then I realised, it was not a dream.

I could hear different types of laugh
I started to get scared,
I started to float up and I land on a cloud
I fell further and further until I landed
And then I saw it
It was not an it but a him
It was me.
I suddenly woke up.

Shyam Vithlani (13)
Hartshill School

MOTHER?

I love you mother
We are together
You are so special
So kind and thoughtful
Special and kind
Love you always
Till the end of time.

Lindsey Barnes (12)
Hartshill School

A Dark Alley

When I walk past the train station
at night I hear the last bird tweet
and then the owl starts to hoot
and then it sounds awfully quiet.
Then I walk on a little
then I see the dark alley.
I take a slow
slow
walk down that alley
that alley is like a cold black room.
Every corner I see I would wonder
what is around that deadly corner.
Then I go round the corner and
there's nothing really there.
then I'm out of that alley
I don't feel so scared.

Natasha Perkins (12)
Hartshill School

A Scary Night

In the middle of the night,
When the clock struck twelve
And the trees were rattling on the window,
The wind was like ghostly voices howling in the night
The owls were going *whooo whooo*
I was very scared I wouldn't dare go out,
The room went silent . . .
So I went upstairs
I got into bed and I went to sleep.

Martin Hartshorn (11)
Hartshill School

FATHER CHRISTMAS

First we welcome snow,
And the snowmen being built.
Then we got ready too,
Hear the jingling of the bells.
Early in the evening no sunshine in sight,
Rudolph sets off with Santa Claus.

Christmas is coming,
Hear us shout.
Rudolph sets off with Santa Claus and the gifts,
If we are good,
Santa promises toys,
To all the girls and boys,
Making Christmas jolly,
All we need to do first is just to fall asleep.

Colin Mullins (11)
Hartshill School

THE GHOST

I linger around in haunted places,
Pulling ghastly, ghostly faces.
The clock has struck at 12:00 midnight,
And I am ready to give humans a fright.
Without my head, I am very thrilling,
I would say I'm quite spine-chilling.
I wonder what it would be like to be alive again,
Instead, I'm under soil in the cold pouring rain.
I didn't think my life would end so soon, never.
So I will just close my eyes and sleep in my grave
      Forever.

Trisha Stallard (11)
Hartshill School

OMAGH BOMBING

We were sent to the opposite end of the street,
There was word of a bomb,
When we got there we all stood around talking.
Then out of the blue the sound of an explosion,
I turned around and to my horror,
I saw buildings crumbling, fires forming
And cars being tossed to the side like toys.
Running towards the chaos
I came across a hand protruding from the rubble,
I cleared away the debris and there
Lying on the floor was a young girl,
She looked only seven and her T-shirt was stained
Crimson with blood from the gash in her side.
I felt for her pulse,
There was none,
She was dead.

David Yates (13)
Hartshill School

GHOST OF TIME

One day or in other words, one cold night,
Snoopy the little ghost was on trial.
Being a ghastly pain again
As usual scaring everyone
Then he got sprayed, he fell down
'Ohh! I think I'm dead' he laughed.
Then very naughtily shouted 'Boo!'
And then the man who had sprayed him ran down
The road never to be seen again.
'That's enough of him' he shouted.

Shani Coulton (11)
Hartshill School

THE OMAGH BOMBING!

I woke up with dust and mud in my face,
My eyes felt old as they slowly opened.
The air smelt musty and damp,
The sky was grey
The clouds were full of smoke.
It suddenly just went dark
But the few flames kept the light from
running away.

My body was stiff and I couldn't move.
I slowly moved my head to see where
my body was.
I was covered in bricks from a collapsed school
I could hear the sound of a baby crying,
And a woman moaning in anger.
Children scattered like buildings that kept
falling and falling.
Mothers worried whether their children will live,
therefore, I may not, because my eyes
are getting weaker and weaker and then suddenly
slipped away from me and my mind went blank.

Laura Kent (13)
Hartshill School

COLD AND ALL ALONE

It's cold and dark
I'm all alone.
I'm standing in an alleyway
Cold as a stone.

It's 10 o'clock in the park
I can hear the trees,
Shaking in the wind
The wind gives me shivers as it whistles.

As the swings swing on their own
A ghostly spirit
Draws nearer,
I'm cold and all alone.

Emma McIver (11)
Hartshill School

THOUGHTS OF OMAGH

As I sat in my class,
       a thought went through my head,
the people of Omagh,
       just lying there dead.

Their loved ones are crying,
       they're hurting so bad,
as the victims just suffer,
       feeling so sad.

The funeral strikes me,
       on Sunday at one,
I look at their faces,
       their happiness gone.

The people spread flowers,
       as the coffins are lowered,
the tears are flooding,
       as the families are buried.

Why did it happen
       what did they do
when would it stop?
       Nobody knew.

Laura Ashby (13)
Hartshill School

THE BOMB

We all ran to the high street where we thought we were safe.
We all huddled together in our groups of family and friends,
Waiting for the signal to say we could return to our homes.
All of a sudden there was a big bang
and bodies went flying everywhere.
There was screaming and shouting with cries of pain.
The flames went shooting in the air with smoke and rubble
showering down on us.

There was a really loud scream that was suddenly cut short.
I opened my eyes to see myself surrounded by brick and glass.
I tried to move my legs but there was no feeling in them.
I looked down to see my legs twisted the wrong way,
it was disgusting.
Trapped under a large piece of rubble I saw my sister
She was crying out my name.
Ignoring the pain, I dragged myself over and comforted her.
I looked around and saw the destruction.
People all around me were crying.
I couldn't help anyone and cried myself to sleep while waiting for help.

Clare Taylor (13)
Hartshill School

NIGHT

It was night
And the moon was shining on some
Beautiful flowers
At night it is cold
And the trees sway from side to side
In the cold wind
The leaves rustle in the wind.

Jennifer Towers (11)
Hartshill School

OMAGH

Running towards the deadly bomb,
but not knowing, not thinking . . .
until it happened.
Lives ended, dreams shattered and hopes gone,
All in a second.
Screams and cries were bells ringing through
the streets of Omagh.
Fear and pain dominated them and blood
stained them.
For weeks after, flowers were laid,
Red roses like broken hearts and white
lilies like the mourning.
If only they could unite and put everyone's
minds to rest - give the people of Ireland some hope
And build their wall of dreams again.

Laura McAdam (13)
Hartshill School

MY FOUR FAVOURITE FRIENDS

I have four favourite friends,
Laura, Emma, Kerry and Sarah
Laura's loud she's always proud
That's what friends are for.
Emma she hates the rain and is a brain.
Kerry she's good at sports
And loves her dog Steff.
Sarah when we leave her out
She goes in a mardy.

Heather Yates (11)
Hartshill School

DREAM

Welcome to your dream,
Yes I'm here,
Welcome to your dream,
Come closer,
It's a dream not a nightmare,
Why can't you see my face you ask,
Well it's your dream,
You imagine it,
Are you still scared?
Well go explore . . .
Nothing can happen,
It's your dream . . .
Change it,
If you like . . .
Well as I said . . .
Welcome to your dream . . .

Anna Hyams (13)
Hartshill School

A POEM ABOUT IRELAND

The sun was shining in the sky,
Summer carnival was in full swing,
Suddenly there was a big bang,
Then there were very loud screams.
The sky filled up with smoke and dust,
Everybody cleared and I saw the blood,
Trickling towards the drains.
Soon after I heard the sirens.
The horror still hangs in the air,
Like a very thick, dark, cold autumn fog.

Graham Collins (13)
Hartshill School

TROUBLED IRELAND

The IRA is a terrible thing,
My home gutted because of their bomb.
Why do they do this? I don't know.
I hate them, what's left of my family hates them.
I don't know why they pick on us,
It isn't fair on our children.
It was only two seconds but it wiped out my family.
Gruesome was the scene - bodies, blood, people,
Screaming panic.
True panic was the scene, 26 dead, 20 children.
Almost one generation wiped out.
The single blast left a bigger hole than the bombsite,
Bigger than the hole in the people's hearts
The biggest hole was in our future generation.

David Bates (13)
Hartshill School

ANIMALS

Animals big or small,
Be they elephants or giraffes which are tall.
They don't deserve to be hunted for a prize,
And bigger the size, doesn't mean bigger the prize.
We don't need to kill elephants for their ivory or little animals
for their fur.
Be it a he or a her.
A life is precious, pure and perfect until, that gunshot . . . !
Those cubs have no mother slowly starving.
But then a saviour is born, whose heart cries out for these animals.
Who are being killed like wildfire.
Soon there will be *no* more animals for us to care for.

Natalie Gilder (13)
Hartshill School

The Ghostly House

As I walked into a cold and ghostly room,
I shivered at the thought of being here.
I walked and I walked until I came to an old,
rusty door.
As I opened the creeky door, the echo scared me
away.
I ran and I ran, then I suddenly stopped.
I turned, I walked as slow as a slug.
Then I heard voices that scared me to death,
they were saying,
'Turn back, turn back'
So I turned back and headed for the door.

When I got out,
the house crumbled into tiny, tiny biscuits
and I never set sight on that horrible, scary
house again.

Lindsay Tynan (13)
Hartshill School

Christmas

Christmas morning happy and full of hope,
This special day is great for the Pope.
I am so excited about this day,
My mum opens her present, a box of Milk Tray.
This is the day, the best of all,
I know my relatives will come round to call.
I rip off the paper from my gifts,
This special day gives everybody a happy lift.

David Monteith (13)
Hartshill School

PUZZLE

Every person is a puzzle,
We live together in a perfect world,
Until a piece of puzzle,
Dries up and curls.

People are starved,
Hungry and alone,
Their lives are carved,
When they are ill they do not moan.

Every piece of this game,
Deserves a life,
To live their name,
And not a life,
To be starved.
A life not to be halved,
By an unhuman flu,
A life to do,
What they want to do.

Kay Percival (14)
Hartshill School

I AM ALONE IN THIS WORLD

I am black, you are white,
I am alone in this world,
Like the moon in the sky and the setting of the sun.
With my twisted back and lonely thoughts,
I am alone in this world.
Why do you ignore me for I am the same as you?
Soon, in time you will realise this,
I am alone in this world.

Matthew Glover (15)
Hartshill School

WALES

Land of peace, of heaven,
A country of ancient Celts,
Worshipping dragons, with skin like gold.

Now forgotten,
Now only peace and beauty remain,
No more are Celtic priests,
Praying to forgotten Gods.
No more are Druids,
Teaching apprentices the once ways.

Where have they gone,
Why have they gone,
Will they return?
No one knows.
In this land of peace, of heaven.

James Wilson (14)
Hartshill School

A LIFE OF ONE BIG MOAN

He's been hit in the back from the hoof of a horse,
He walks around the barn like running around a course,
His friends are the horses,
His home is the barn,
Hay he sleeps on,
And socks he darns.
No one to talk to,
All alone,
Just a different colour,
A life of one big moan.

Aimeé Oakley (15)
Hartshill School

Macabre Mansion

The door swung open,
The floorboards creaked,
And at the door there stood,
A tall and ghostly creature.

He whispered,
'Enter,' and I did as he said,
But as I entered the horror-filled hallway,
I knew I should not have come.

The room felt like a freezer,
And the floor was a carpet of dead rats,
And the crunching, creaking sound that I made,
Sent a shiver running down my spine.

As soon as he had disappeared,
I wandered into the next dark room,
For I had a sudden, overpowering urge,
To explore this intriguing mansion.

'Drip, drip' was the noise that came from the ceiling,
And I felt a little warmth,
For one small noise,
Is better than no noise at all.

I stood glued to the spot,
When a figure appeared in the doorway,
And I knew that he was back,
And ready to kill for life.

I ran out of the adjacent doorway,
And ran until I could run no more,
And as I reached the cool fresh air,
I gave one long exhausted scream for help.

Sarah King (13)
Hartshill School

THE DIANA EFFECT

A tear fell from the heart of the world.

Her outstanding elegance along with grace,
Her aching beauty puts a smile on your face.
You hit rock-bottom,
The agony puts a hole deep in your soul.
A shiver tickles down my spine,
Like a freezing ice cube drenched in wine.
Kicking, cursing, crying, an horrendous potion,
A barrelled waterfall of emotion.
After two exemplary specimens of life,
The paparazzi only brought her anguish and strife.
Her personality crawled with warmth and happiness,
Although her personal being was overcome with distress.
Respected by millions a remarkable story,
A true Princess in all her glory.

For England's Rose, a tear fell from the heart of the world.

Natalie Osadciw (14)
Hartshill School

THE FLAME

I sat on the Indonesian rug,
Feeling the warmth of the coal fire next to me.
I was drowning in the heat, like I was locked in a steamy sauna,
Gazing into the mysterious flame.

Colours of red, orange and yellow lit up the darkened room,
In which I lay.
I felt alone,
The burning fire, my only companion.

Smoke rising up through the soot-blocked chimney,
Began to fill up the room.
The fire began to die,
As the last lump of coal turned to ashes.

I started to choke with the fumes,
All went black, as if a dark spirit had stolen my soul.
But I could still see the blazing fire beyond my eyelids,
My only friend began to hurt me, as it burnt me to a cinder.

Nick Turner (14)
Hartshill School

FOOTBALL

Football, football.
Great, great goal.

Football, football,
Scored by Scholes.

Football, football,
Run the wing.

Football, football,
Score and sing.

Football, football,
Don't let it in.

Football, football,
We're going to win.

Football, football,
We've just won.

Mark Reason (13)
Hartshill School

A Night To Remember

The night was dark and misty,
I walked home alone that night.
I sang as I walked past the church,
The graveyard shone, scary and bright.
The leaves scrunched beneath my feet,
My feet were really wet and soggy.
I ran part of the way through the woods,
The sky began to get foggy.
I bumped into my friend from school,
She seemed a little weird,
She pointed behind her back,
And there it stood,
The ghost I'd always feared.

Paula Piff (13)
Hartshill School

Crooks

Sitting alone with no one to talk to,
No one to talk to and nothing to do.
I only have a few books,
And I read the same books over and over.
People are scared of the colour of my skin,
They fear me because I'm different,
But underneath I'm just like them.
It makes me so angry when people call me names,
They don't understand I have feelings just like them.
They don't realise how much it hurts,
All I want is someone to talk to,
Someone to feel the pain.

Chris Skyner (15)
Hartshill School

UNFINISHED BUSINESS

I walked up the path of an ancient house,
And knocked on the old brown door.
I peered inside as it opened,
Then stepped inside.
I smelt a smoky, choking smell,
And I tried not to breathe it in.
It was dark in the hall,
So a candle I lit,
To see the way around.
I climbed the great staircase
And walked through passages,
Until I reached my destiny.
An old, mouldy cardboard box
Stood before me.
I opened the lid, and in it was
A sphere, with a button at the side.
I pressed the button, and with a whirr,
It opened, and concealed within was a shell.
Was the crystal coconut, my only dream.
I picked it up and ran for my life,
Bt, as I got to the old brown door,
An invisible 'thing' stopped me.
I pushed and shoved, and shoved and pushed,
But alas, I was trapped.
Trapped! Trapped forever!
Doomed to guard the coconut,
For now I am dead, just an *invisible* spirit,
Forced to carry out someone else's
Unfinished business.

Gayle Johnson (14)
Hartshill School

THE SEASIDE

The silk blue sky,
Is a mystery to one's eye.
Is as the silk-blue sea
That lies there in front of me.

Sitting there on the sandy beach,
The crystal waters in my reach.
Lying there looking up to the sky,
Watching the seagulls fly on by.

Lying down sweltering hot,
My skin as tight as a strong, long knot.
Through the day,
The boats begin to drift away.

Through the day,
The boats begin to drift away.
Everyone starts to wave,
And in they go to a dark, gloomy cave.

Later on in comes the tide,
All the fish begin to hide.
The waves abanging and crashing around,
The rocks would never be there to be found.

Kirsty Yates (11)
Hartshill School

OLD MCBERT

Old McBert had a pheasant,
It flapped its wings all day,
But when McBert wasn't present,
The pheasant flew away.

It flapped its wings all day,
It travelled four different ways,
But when it got home,
McBert was a clone,
And for pheasant meat he did crave.

David Miles (13)
Hartshill School

BABIES

The small child is born
You see its first yawn
Is it a girl or is it a boy
Or would it be a lot quieter?
If it was a toy
It makes more noise than a pup
And it likes to wake you up
You give it all your love
After all, it came from above
It has a mum and a dad
It makes you happy and sad
The child starts to moan
When its first tooth has grown
First it walks
And then it talks
You have to change the babies nappy
This does not make it very happy
The baby gets sad
It makes you mad
But best of all
It's precious and small.

Louise Brown (13)
Hartshill School

THE SEA POEM

I'm sitting on a sandy beach
Looking far and wide,
Looking at the silk-blue sea
Waiting for the tide.

The sand is cold and very damp
With pebbles here and there,
The water's getting near to me
But I just don't really care.

The silk-blue blanket in front of me
Is such a great delight,
I could sit here on the sandy beach
And stare at it all night.

The shells buried beneath the sand
Tickle my bare, pink feet,
The rhythmical whooshing,
Is the sea's lonely beat.

The waves' crashing movement
Sounds like shattered glass,
I watch the colours of the fish
As I see them pass.

The moon is now appearing
In the evening sky,
So now until tomorrow
I'll say goodnight and bye.

Christine Yeomans (11)
Hartshill School

CLOUDS

I gazed up to the cotton wool-like clouds,
Wishing into the sky that I could be a part of life up there.
I see the birds gliding up above my head,
and hope that one day I could be a part of the freedom they have.
The clouds float gracefully along the blue sky,
Patched with their whiteness and purity.
The clouds start to darken and become an angry grey form in the sky.
I saw splashes of rain start to fall and the birds clear the sky in search
of shelter.
I stood alone with heavy drops of rain trickling down my back,
soaking through my clothes.
Suddenly a shout broke into my thoughts,
It was my auntie standing at the light-filled window beckoning me
to return to the warmth of our home and the cosy flame-filled log fire.
I drifted into a relaxing sleep and the sun shone again.

Laura Skyner (13)
Hartshill School

GOALKEEPER

I'm the greatest goalkeeper
In the world.
The *'best'*
The *'best'*
All the fans shouting, screaming for me.
Oh what a save!
Brilliant save!
Great save!
The *'best'*
The *'best'*.

(What, they've scored!)

Jamie Barr (13)
Hartshill School

NED KELLY THE BANDIT

Ned Kelly was a bandit,
A bum some would say.
He wore an iron mask in the
Middle of the day.
He robbed the rich to save the poor,
Found Ned Kelly on the floor.

Bonfire night.
Fireworks bang in the sky.
I heard a noise, it frightened me.
Rain falls on Bonfire night,
Everybody drenched.

When it bangs, I jump high
Over the fire into the sky.
Roads are busy.
Knocking on some windows,
Saw someone was telling me off.

Emma Louise Bennett (14)
Hartshill School

CROOKS

He sits in his room,
No one to talk to,
Everybody avoids him because he is black.

He thinks 'Why me, what have I done,
Why does no one talk to me,
Why do they treat me like an animal?
I can read and write so why does it matter what colour I am?

Darren Brooks (16)
Hartshill School

BEDTIME

It's time to go to sleep,
Go to the land of dreams.
Think of all the bunnies,
Princesses and fairy queens.
Put your head on your pillow,
Snuggle down in your quilt.
Cuddle up to teddy,
Then gently close your eyes.

Danielle Jack (11)
Hartshill School

CROOKS

Sitting alone with no one to talk to,
I sit and read my books.
People are scared by the colour of my skin,
Don't they know I'm just like them?
It makes me so angry when they call me names,
They just don't realise how much it hurts,
All I want is someone to talk to,
Someone to share the pain.

Sam Swami (15)
Hartshill School

SUMMER HOLIDAYS

The summer holidays are good fun,
You get to see every one,
Your friends and family are off away,
Let's throw a party - hip, hip hooray!

Melissa Day (13)
Hartshill School

GRANDAD

Me and my grandad
Were best mates,
I saw him every day,
And now he's gone.
He was always there to listen,
We had lots of good times together,
Playing chess, playing cards,
(Even though I could never win)
Now he's gone,
And I miss him.
I can't play chess or cards with him anymore,
But I still talk to him,
And I know he listens.

James Rathbone (13)
Hartshill School

SUMMER NIGHTS

The summer nights are always the greatest
Watching the sun softly go down
Like a teardrop down your face.
Your fears and worries blow away with the wind,
Nothing to concern you.
The whole world fits into place.
I love the summer nights,
How the birds make themselves a nice new home
to settle down for the night.
To wake up bright and early the next day and
feed their chicks.
I love the summer nights.

Jenny Rowson (13)
Hartshill School

THE STREETS

The streets are cold, wet and lonely,
Men and women hurry past on their way to a warm home,
I smile at them and they look back as if I don't belong.

The sky slowly darkens,
A thick mist forms in the road,
The street lamps twinkle off the wet sidewalk and light my path,
Everywhere is silent and empty, like my heart.

As I walk my footsteps echo off buildings,
Houses tower over me,
I gaze into the night sky and look at the stars,
They shimmer in the darkness.

The wind, wildly whooshed around me,
I turned a corner,
My home was in sight,
Not a home like others,
Mine is cold, wet and hard.

Emma Ashby (13)
Hartshill School

OUR WEE SCHOOL!

Our wee school is a great wee school,
It's made of bricks and plaster,
The only thing that we don't like,
Is our wee bald headmaster.
He goes to the pub on a Saturday night,
He goes to church on Sunday,
To pray to God to give him strength
To murder us on a Monday!

Jemma Dunnachie (12)
Hartshill School

THE BUNGALOW

The house is old and rotten,
cold, damp and empty.
No one lives there, but
the sound of footsteps still haunts this
deserted house.

The house has no stairs,
no upstairs, downstairs only.
This place is not a palace,
no home, but giving a little
tender loving care, it
could be someone's pride and joy.
This house's garden has a lawn
its waist high with the weeds,
it has a car, quite a new one,
it's a Fiesta 1.1.

This house is no living space
but it once was someone's home and
now they're gone, the house
stands there alone.

Matthew Brown (14)
Hartshill School

BONFIRE NIGHT

Fireworks shooting in the sky,
Some are soaring very high.
Some blue, some red, some green,
Some that I have never seen.

People staring into the night,
Others sat and watched with fright.
Sparklers glowing in the dark,
Leaving a light as their trademark.

The bonfire glowing all alone,
Some people started heading home.
The Guy Fawkes doll burning away,
Look at that, some people might say.

The coloured dots falling down,
Some of them fell to the ground.
The fire was now dying away,
We'll just have to wait for another day.

Helen Holt (14)
Hartshill School

SMELLY SOCKS

Smelly socks are everywhere
under my bed and anywhere.
Especially on my brother's feet
well that just isn't a very good treat.

When you're lying in bed
your smelly socks are there.
When you throw your clothes in the wash
your socks may give you a scare.

Because smelly socks are everywhere
even on your bedroom chair.
Your dad's socks, well all I can say
is don't go near, just keep away.

If you do you'll have a shock
and won't want to see another sock.
Because your dad's socks are the worst of all
they're that bad, they can me you bawl.

Rebecca Ashby (13)
Hartshill School

TASTY CAKE

As I crept downstairs,
To peep at the cake,
Not a sound do I try to make.
What's that sound?
Who's around?
If it's my mum,
I'll surely get done.
Quick let's hide,
The noise is from outside.
I creep back to the cake again,
A tree branch taps on the windowpane.
Into the icing my finger dips,
It is then placed onto my lips.
The cake disappears slowly,
Eventually it's all gone.
Oh no, I've eaten my whole birthday cake.
Mum appears looking cross,
My bums gets slapped,
I get sent back to bed,
Not that I'm bothered,
It's my cake anyway.

Lorna Tarplin (13)
Hartshill School

SPORTS

Rugby tackle
The mud is great
All over the shirts
So rugby is great

Football is fun
Football is great
Football is so cool
After you celebrate

Cricket is fun
But bowling the ball is better fun
I love batting
And also running

Tennis is cool
But I love the rackets
And also the balls
Because they make a racket.

Alan Lapworth (12)
Hartshill School

FOOTBALL

Football is my favourite sport.
Football is my favourite game.
Football is so good
You get to roll in the mud.

Football is such fun.
You can watch it in the sun.
Football can also be a pain
When you have to play it in the rain.

Football shorts and football tops,
All different colours in the shops.
Some are small and some are large,
Different prices they all charge.

Football is a real good sport
Loved by people of every sort.
All sorts of players in different strips
All fighting for the championships.

Sam Hands (12)
Hartshill School

BABIES

Babies are cute, cute as can be
They always throw around and mess up their tea
They sleep in a cot
So you should sing them a song
But when they fill their nappies, oh what a pong!
They cry in the night
They cry in the day
But when they awake they always want to play
When their teeth start to come through
All they want to do is chew, chew, chew
When they're asleep they look so sweet
But in the morning they shout and scream
Oh no, not again.

Emma Spittle (12)
Hartshill School

I NEED YOU

I need you more and more each day,
I cannot believe you left to run away.
Please come back, I need you so,
Tell me you still love me and that it will always flow.
Why did you go? I thought you still cared.
With you, my love I always shared.
Don't tell me our love is dead,
Every day a tear is shed.
Please come back, I love you so much,
Never a bond has been so strong as such.
Please come back, every day I cry,
Don't say that this is goodbye.

Carly Slane (13)
Hartshill School

HALLOWE'EN

Hallowe'en is scary
Hallowe'en is fun
Hallowe'en makes you scream
That's why it's fun.

Brooms and witches haunt the night
I like to give people a very big fright.

Trick or Treating is so cool
But the sweets make us drool
But all night those kids fight
But some people want some quiet at night.

Black cats miaow in the night
at the back of the brooms.
Which gives us a fright
But it usually starts a fight.

Michael Lapworth (12)
Hartshill School

SPRINGTIME

Spring is a time of happiness,
As the new buds pop out of the ground.
The temperature starts to rise,
There's colourful flowers all around.
The trees have new foliage,
With the wind blowing, making the trees
wave goodbye to winter.
The seeds now need sowing.
The children come out to play,
after being snuggled up in bed.

Amy Matts (13)
Hartshill School

SLEEP!

Close your eyes,
Listen so deeply,
The gentle harmony voice,
Singing so weakly,
Close your eyes.

The whimper of a baby,
Going back to sleep,
Maybe,
No crying, screaming,
Howling, shouting,
Just the gentle voice
Close your eyes,
And go to sleep,
Goodnight.

Kate Brown (13)
Hartshill School

THE WAR

I am in the air raid shelter, dark at night,
Not one light I can see.
I can hear the sound of guns shooting away
and the sound of children screaming.
I am frightened in case I die.
I am frightened of being caught
and being locked away for the rest of my life.
Why can't people love each other and
always be there for one another.
If people did, this wouldn't be happening right now.

Joanne Harborne (13)
Hartshill School

CHRISTMAS

Winter is coming
All around snow will fall on the ground
Children love to play day by day
Having fun all day.

Shops will get full at this time of year
Christmas is for girls and boys
Lots and lots of lovely toys
All day long.

Time off school, we'll all get bored
Till Christmas is here
And we get our new gear
For our next year.

With our new toys and all our clothes
We can go back to school
And not look a fool.

James Power (12)
Hartshill School

HALLOWE'EN

In the dark, dark, dark night
You don't know who's about
Looking, looking side to side
Looking, looking up and down
And then bang! Bang!
The birds flying, flying out of trees
Chirping, chirping at the noise
Then you remember it's the
Fifth of November.

Ryan Miller (12)
Hartshill School

HOMELESS

In the cold and damp,
Sitting there,
My head in my knees,
People going by with disgust
and pity written on their faces.
I expect nobody knows what it feels like
to be abandoned by the world,
not to be cared for or not to be
something special.
Maybe one day the mists of time
will open the eyes of the world,
not just to help me, but others in need.

Emily Whopples (13)
Hartshill School

HALLOWE'EN

I looked out of my window at night
What I saw gave me a fright
There was a witch on her broom
She saw me watching from my room
She came towards me to cast a spell
And into her cauldron I fell
I really did not want to die
Then away she flew into the sky.

Gary Hughes (13)
Hartshill School

THE TORNADO

The tornado destructively meandered,
destroying everything it touched.
A cyclone, a typhoon,
a whirlwind, a storm.

Hopping over a long stretch
of ground,
Huge, fast, strong, angry,
a natural disaster.

Lee Trembeth (13)
Hartshill School

MY SISTER'S BIRTHDAY
(For Trisha)

Ten times she's showed us her list,
'For crying out loud,
I think we get the gist,'
I howled

She keeps saying,
'Ooh, it's almost here!'
However, I am just praying,
That she's not like this next year.

Finally, the day arrives,
The letters on the mat,
Cars pulls up on the drive,
And she's dancing in her party hat.

The morning after the night before,
I am made to clear up,
Party hats on the floor,
Parts of a paper cup.

My sister is playing with her stuff,
I ask her for a go,
Oh well, that's just tough,
The answer will always be *'No!'*

Leigh Stallard (13)
Hartshill School

STREET LIFE

There he was sitting all alone,
with nowhere to go, not even
a home.
His messy long brown hair,
his straggly clothes,
his dirty feet especially his toes.
It's just not fair to see him there,
everybody walking by, not
seeming to care.
What will happen in the
winter when the snow is on the
ground.
Will he still be there, or will
he be found.
What about his birthday
and Christmas too.
What will he get,
nothing that's true.
So what shall I do
now, so he's not
sitting there
sad? I'll give
him some
company,
so I don't
feel
bad.

Nicola Hadley (13)
Hartshill School

THE BOY

There he was a tall figure,
Walking a short black dog.
As I strolled along the muddy field,
Spying through the fog.
As he lifted his head and smiled at me,
Very hesitantly.
I looked in his great big eyes,
Which looked right back at me.
He motioned his hand with a come-on sign,
Which I took with a happy sigh.
Just as it was getting interesting,
His dog let out a cry.

Charlotte Brindley (14)
Hartshill School

WHY OH WHY DOES IT HAVE TO BE ME!

Why oh why does it have to be me,
the one that gets stung by a bumblebee.

Why oh why does it have to be me,
the one that falls over and hurts my knee.

Why oh why does it have to be me,
the one that has to climb that tree.

Why oh why does
it have to be
me!

Cheryl Fox (13)
Hartshill School

THE STARS

Stars are like diamonds
Twinkling through the night
Sparkling, flashing when the time is right
When the night ends, the sun comes up
The stars go down
Ready for the next night.

Hayley Jones (12)
Hartshill School

A BALLOON RIDE

Rising higher above the clouds,
Watching the world like a bird,
Floating with the wind,
Soaring higher and higher,
Watching the world disappear below.

Ryan Ashby (13)
Hartshill School

THE GAME OF GOLF

Golf is a game of skill,
overcoming bunkers, lakes and the odd hill.
Makes it satisfying to complete a round,
even if your score is not a happy sound.

Golfers wear strange hats and funny socks,
this enables them to miss any rocks.
So they can achieve a reasonable score,
and so they have the right to say *fore!*

By hitting a small ball in a hole,
brings as much fun as scoring a goal.
You can use a putter, iron or a wood,
but remember to try and keep out of the mud!

The course is designed to be full of traps,
but there are short cuts if you find the gaps.
Use the wrong club and it could be all over,
you could smash the window of a very nice Rover!

Chris Sharp (15)
Henley High School

THE END

The sky was dark, the stars stood still,
The earth just waited for the final kill.
The trees stood to attention, each in a row,
The clouds didn't rain and the wind didn't blow.
The grass stopped dancing and plants froze cold,
The air just whispered and they were told,
The time had come, the final frontier,
The weeks have ended, no more months, or years
The countdown is now, until the end,
The money means nothing and even time can't mend,
The devastation caused, the death and pain,
The fighting is over, not to be seen again,
The only thing's left is what you see,
The last standing flower, the last standing tree,
The final race, colour, religion and creed,
The final breath lost because of power and greed,
The Armageddon is now, it has come to take away,
The only hour of the very last day,
The world sat still, no sound or light,
The first day of the last, when the future took flight.

Carrie Laity (15)
Henley High School

Monday Morning Blues

It's a dreadful Monday morning,
It's raining and dull outside,
I hear my mom shouting my name,
I just want to run and hide.

I get myself washed and dressed,
And make my way downstairs,
Nothing's going right today,
I'm already getting grey hairs.

I'm on my way to school now,
Trying to keep awake,
Thinking of all the things to do,
I'm getting a major headache.

I've now arrived in the building of work,
And I'm trying to be polite,
To all my friends and teachers,
Trying to do things right.

I've now reached first lesson,
Another three of these,
Learning about all sorts,
Roll on Friday please.

I now know that I've got one day left,
Which leads on steadily to a week,
To get up every morning at 6 on the dot,
Where I'm becoming incredibly weak.

I've come to a good conclusion,
To ban school altogether,
Then you can do just what you like,
And sleep whatever the weather.

Katie Herrick (15)
Henley High School

THE WEST BROM

Match day arrives and the tension builds,
A train ride to the ground and with excitement I'm filled,
As I go through the turnstiles the crowd I hear cry,
'The West Brom, the West Brom.'

I take my seat amongst the devoted crowd,
The teams make their way into the ground,
And the crowd are on their feet singing aloud,
'The West Brom, the West Brom.'

The ball on the spot, the referee blows,
The match under way, the players on their toes,
Lee Hughes receives the ball as the crowd chants,
'The West Brom, the West Brom.'

Lee Hughes cuts past the defender with finesse,
The crowd are adoring the skills he possess,
He strikes the ball with a thump as the crowd go wild, 1-0,
'The West Brom, the West Brom.'

The defence may lapse but Miller is there,
And the skills of Kilbane, with such amazing flair,
Kilbane delivers the ball and Fab is there, 2-0,
'The West Brom, the West Brom.'

The final whistle brings a 2-0 win,
The crowd have their arms in the air,
The blue and white stripes gave the visitors a 'mare,
'The West Brom, the West Brom.'

Chris Freeman (15)
Henley High School

Dreamscape

I'm walking through the clouds so white,
As I travel through my dreams this night,
Living out my fantasies, fun and wild,
Cowering from the nightmares as they stalk my streets,
Covering myself in blackness, like a frightened child.

How could it have started so serenely before,
And now this frightful spectre is knocking at my mind's door?
So full of tranquillity, but now as dead as my calm,
Which refuse to return with its soothing balm,
To heal my abused soul from this tormenting cycle.

Around and around my dreams do go,
Though nightmares in truth they be,
For every night, no matter how I try,
The scenes return to haunt my sleep,
And slowly warp my mind into insanity.

Now, madness all the world doth seem,
All my life spent in endless pain,
And every time I close my eyes, my lips issue their sorrowful scream.
The shadows return, my mind does burn,
With the souls of those that died at my hand.

I had never wanted to kill, or even to follow such an order,
But we all knew what was expected when we reached the border.
Murder was what it was, though they said it was defence of the good,
Innocent lives were those that were taken, not those that were
the enemy,
We had no choice, just set the guns a-firing, when told we should.

Many are buried in lands unknown,
Others just left where they fell,
The soil and time took their pain and guilt of such a season,
But for those who lived the dreams condemned,
The dreams took their toll, and wreaked their revenge.

Lucy Swift (15)
Henley High School

TEACHERS

Teachers think they are funny people,
As they think they are the best,
But the only funny thing about them,
Is the way they tend to dress.

They sit at their desks,
With the nice comfy chairs,
And pretend they know what they're on about,
But if you asked them a question,
On another subject,
They wouldn't have a clue.

Then they think they are brilliant,
By not letting the kids to the loo,
You should have gone at lunchtime,
That's the excuse, that used to be used,
So they have to sit and wait there,
Until five past two.

At the end of the day,
What do they do?
Do they have lives of their own?
Or do they sleep at school,
And wait for us to return, the next day.

Laura Compton (15)
Henley High School

PEELING PAINT

Peeling paint.
It's clinging for its life,
On a dull, dreary, lifeless wall.
Every once in a while,
A piece flakes off,
And falls to the carpet,
Like a snowflake,
A gift from heaven,
Who is dancing on her way to the ground.
Time ages the wall,
Which is barren,
And exposed.
Showing that ghostly,
Dingy coloured paint,
There was before.
That paint is given a second life,
For a while,
Until the sun,
Who is unrelenting,
In his powerful burst of light and heat,
And is on his quest,
To destroy that paint,
So that it slowly floats,
Whirls and swirls,
To the floor,
Where it dies,
And is buried,
In the black bag of death.

Lucie Wheatcroft (15)
Henley High School

FOOTBALL

A single whistle blown by a single person,
Suddenly excites hundreds of thousands of people,
Twenty-two players running around after one object,
Their objective,
To get it between two posts and a crossbar,
A simple concept,
A simple game,
Teams competing against each other,
To win a prestigious title,
And the right to say they're number one,
Devoted fans,
Who eat,
Sleep and breathe it,
All combined make the most popular sport worldwide,
Football.

Rebecca Laing (15)
Henley High School

WHAT IF . . .

As I look around and feel trapped not knowing what to do,
I imagine myself in a bubble.
What if I tried to get out?
What if I fell or would I land on my feet?
What if I stayed but felt trapped forever?
What if I escaped but found I had made the wrong choice?
But if I made the right one, is it what I really want or best for me?
What if somebody popped it for me and caught my body and soul?
I would be safe and no longer trapped.
Who knows what the future holds for me.
But that I control mine.

Hannah Smalley (15)
Henley High School

THE TREE

A little girl went through a wood,
Not caring what she'd see,
She skipped and played along the path,
And bumped straight into a tree.
Back she fell onto the floor,
She really was quite thrown,
She'd walked this path the other day,
Since then the tree had grown.
The tree grew taller as she watched,
Bigger each bough became,
It stretched right up into the sky,
She'd never seen the same.
Slowly she got to her feet,
Really quite on edge,
She did not know what next she'd see,
And backed into a hedge.
She started to get quite alarmed,
This really wasn't right,
She'd gone out for a pleasant walk,
Not an afternoon of fright.
She really wanted to go home,
But didn't know the way,
None of us have seen her since,
She's out there to this day.

Joanna Hardman (15)
Henley High School

My Night-Time Poem

On a late September night,
A poem I decided I would write.
Outside I went into the gloom,
And waited for my mind to bloom.

I sat down on a wooden chair,
Looked skywards and said a prayer.
I lit a candle, prepared my den,
And began to write with my pen.

Overhead a plane did fly,
But in the night I could not spy.
The sky above was filled with stars,
And round about were sounds of cars.

The sound of blowing trees prevailed,
But never once had it galed.
The cold drew in with its icy finger,
And I knew then I should not linger.

I closed my book, put back my pen,
And slowly took apart my den.
I walked back in and then looked out,
I was now finished without a doubt.

Robert Stone (16)
Henley High School

POEMS

Writing poems just isn't for me,
I leave it all till the last minute,
I'm not very good at them, as you'll see,
And I normally end up binnin' it!

I'm always stuck and up till all hours,
Trying to think what to say,
I don't want to write about my family or flowers,
I just want to go out and play.

If I asked my dad, or even my mum,
'For a poem, what should I write?'
They'll tell me things I've already done,
And it'll always end up in a fight!

So I try and find a title to write,
But my brain is wearing thin,
My pen I now seem to bite,
And that's when the poem goes in the bin.

Now, the bin at this point is full to the brim,
And there's paper all over the floor,
It's now that I find out if I'm really dim,
And if I should quit and head for the door.

It's almost complete,
And not much more to be done,
Just a few more lines, and then write it in neat,
And then I can go out and have fun!

Alistair Barrett (15)
Henley High School

THE GORGON

The village is empty,
Except for one lone child,
And she soon will be no more,
For in the hills and valleys the Gorgon there does prowl,
A beast with teeth as big as castle towers,
And serpents darker than the darkest night for hair,
It beats its leathered wings,
Which are the colour of old blood,
And to its dinner flies.

Swift, silent and deadly,
Is the Gorgon, as it skims over the sky,
Then dives, grabbing its victims,
Seconds later they are no more,
Ground to a mush,
By its powerful teeth,
Wherever the Gorgon goes it leaves behind no life,
Only a pile of gnawed bones.

But where is the man to slay the Gorgon?
Where is the brave, intelligent man?
Where is the man to slay the Gorgon?
No man living could ever do that,
It must be woman v woman,
But who?
Who is cunning enough to slay the Gorgon,
To slay the creature which causes every face to go pale,
Who?
Helen, that is who!
Helen the brave,
Helen the cunning,
Helen to slay the Gorgon!

Ruth MacDonald (12)
Kenilworth School

THE ALIEN FOOTBALLER

The alien footballer was practising for his big match,
although he had broken a bone, he was ready and raring to go.

The alien's eyes were glowing bright and red,
and his jelly head wobbled weirdly.

His eyes were wobbling and his suckers were sucking,
his feet are dynamic,
and his feet are also the shape of football boots.

He has the speed of lightning,
and his mouth is in a funny place.

The final day has come,
and he is dressed in his football kit,
and has cleaned up his bright clean body.
Guess what? He scored a hat-trick and his team won the cup.

Luke Stanley (12)
Kenilworth School

HELP ME

God in heaven hear me pray
As the daylight goes away.
Asking you to watch over me
As I dream and slumber deep.

God in heaven cleanse my soul
Leaving me happy and whole.
When morning comes, help me to be
Good and gentle, more like thee.

Emma Ballard (11)
Kenilworth School

HATRED

They obviously didn't
Understand the word reality.
I couldn't believe it
When I got the telegram.

'Killed in action - Russ Jones' it read
My brother had just been killed
I was just left with the happy memories
Of my brother and I playing.

I can remember
When I used to tell him secrets
He never told anyone else
Not even Mum!

He was always happy and friendly
Unless someone or something had died
He'd always had millions of friends
In the army and at school

He meant a lot to everyone
And now he'll mean even more
I cannot tell you how much
But I know it'll be more after every day.

But now those happy days are over
And so is his life
My heart has never been broken before
But it is now that my brother has died.

Natalie Johnson (11)
Kenilworth School

ZOG

Captain Zog with an evil grin
summoned his son Tin Tin Tin.
His six eyes stared, waddled and glared
and his twenty-six mouths sniggered and jeered.
His little green body wobbled with mirth
as he said to his son 'Let's take over Earth.'
His son, who looked just like him,
said 'Oh yes, what fun, let's go after tea.'
With an army of Groggs they set into space
to conquer Earth and the human race.
The Groggs were thick and not so bright
and didn't get calculations right.
They travelled for fifty million light years
yet near no Earth did they steer.
Until evil Zog and his army of Groggs
landed on the planet Zarog.
The planet was bare without any trees
and all that was there were lumps of cheese.
Tin went to one and proudly said
'Take us to your leader, blockhead.'
The cheese just sat and didn't move,
it was shiny and yellow without any grooves.
Zog cried out 'Oh Louise
these are only slabs of cheese.'
So into space they again did go
until they reached their home sweet home.
'Let's never do that again,' Tin said
'Let's take over Mars instead.'

Elizabeth Harwood (12)
Kenilworth School

SEASONS CHANGING

Summer was a blast
But now it's all past
Autumn is calling
And the leaves are falling.

The rain starts to pour
And the thunder begins to roar
No sooner is it light
Till it's dark at night.

The whistling wind of autumn blows
It's very good for drying clothes
The farmers finish harvesting their crops
Before the rain starts to drop.

Laura McKay (13)
Kenilworth School

SCIENTIST COMPOSING

This person is a bookcase made of autumn wood
He is an orange night life with a vodka in his paw
He drives home like he is in the Bill, but really he is just
a rose
He is a shirt the colour of lemon, the classical scientist
composing his work.

Philip Wiggins (14)
North Leamington School

You Or Me?

Your lips to me are like a freshly sprung rose,
A strong temptation to meet them with mine.
A passionate embrace to strike a pose,
The taste as luscious as mature red wine.
You run your fingers through your long brown locks,
Your olive skin shines with a summer glow;
The women of the town follow in flocks;
I am the one pierced by Cupid's bow.

If only I could feel your loving touch
And be affirmed with spoken words of love,
Then could emotions blossom forth that such,
Astounding love is blessed by God above.
Yet sadly this would seem it cannot be;
Obsession is with self more than with me.

Rebecca Wallace (16)
North Leamington School

Orange Tulip Lamp

This person is an orange tulip lamp.
She is a chocolate dog covered in Coke,
Sitting by a BMW.
Behind Coronation Street, she is whistling her
heart out.
She goes to Scotland once a year and looks
at the little maple tree.
Above the lamp she is sipping Calvin Klein
and eating chocolate.

Rebecca Robbins (11)
North Leamington School

ANGER

Anger is a dark bloody red.
It tastes like boiled mustard and
smells like boiled fish.
It looks like fire or a devil on a stake
and sounds like shouting echoing around.
Anger feels like a thousand pins sticking
in your body.

Fiona Moore (11)
North Leamington School

ORANGE

Burning flames.
Relaxing, burning hot places.
A sweet, long smell.
Round, rolling, big and small.
Juicy, tasty, mouth-watering.
Bursting to open.

Nisha Rai (12)
North Leamington School

WHITE

A smooth blank canvas waiting for
colour to be splashed on.
The sea crashing against great, grey
rocks with seagulls swooping by and
leaving their mark.
Still statues in an empty art gallery.

James White (12)
North Leamington School

ANGER

Anger is red,
A burning fire,
A volcano's lava which bubbles over,
A rough unsanded piece of wood,
A never ending feeling,
It tastes like hot, spicy curry,
Like a river which flows into a
big sea of arguments.

Zoe Millington (12)
North Leamington School

ORANGE

Bright blazing spring sun,
Hot, warm, soft and smooth,
A leaf in autumn crinkled and torn,
Hot deserts burnt and parched,
Joy and gladness burning through.

Richard Evans (12)
North Leamington School

VERMILLION

This is a volcanic rock in a bloody ocean,
The sound of screams in a fiery hole,
The signs of danger,
The flash of the sun,
Watch blood pour, dance and run.

Matthew Lester (12)
North Leamington School

TESTS

Mind blank
Paper blank
Eyes glazed
Desk wobbly

No talking
No messing about
You have one hour to complete the test
Turn here

No 1. Which witch is witch?
Oh simple
That's a witch
And that's not a witch

No. 51. $3.8 + 100 \div 3 \times 5 =$
Aaaaaahhhhhh!
This test is not easy
It's torture

5 minutes left now.
There's too many questions
And not enough time

No. 80. Why did they invent
Numbers more than 50?
To torture us

No. 83. What do you do
At a red light?
'Stop
Papers closed
Pens and pencils down'

I hate tests.

Thomas Barnwell (11)
North Leamington School

CONVERSATION WITH LOVE

I'm trying to fill a void in my life,
I found that was there now I can't have you.
Pain when I think of you slits like a knife,
So what, asked my heart, are you going to do?

I don't know! I moaned to my heart one day.
He sees me, but only my outer shell.
His affections for me I cannot sway,
My life is becoming an empty hell.

It's plain he's unable to see my love.
My heart with impatience says let him know
He fills you with joy like the birdsong above,
Colours your life as the bright flowers below.

But, said my heart, if you don't, then by fate,
He'll go from your life, it will be too late.

Emily Holloway (16)
North Leamington School

THE CASTLE

The thunder was growling,
as the rain whipped,
the mud was like gnarled hands,
the branches on the trees were
like greedy claws,
I was thrown from side to side
with a jerk of the carriage,
in the castle there were werewolves
running round like wild dogs.

Beth Mountford (11)
North Leamington School

THE CASTLE

Leading up the narrow ravine,
heading for the castle,
past the mud which reared out like gnarled hands.
I'm getting closer,
it's hard to see,
the rain is coming down hard,
like rain whipped air,
there it is,
the glistening castle.

The trees have greedy claws,
like monsters,
the castle looks like the cracked ribs of a giant dead lizard,
in a thorny jungle.
Crows fly off like frightened vultures.
The night is as dark as coal-black cellar darkness,
and then I heard it,
the growl of the thunder coming from behind,
the castle.

Rachel Stickley (11)
North Leamington School

THE CASTLE

The castle glared with rain drops glistening.
The shadows swaying grotesquely over the stone walls.
A thorny jungle of briars, mud like gnarled hands.
He lived in a squalor with rubbish and cobwebs.
Rain whipped air and a coal black cellar.

Joanne Burton (11)
North Leamington School

SNAKE

The
  slow
    sly snake
       whispers
         in the
       long
      tall
    reeds
  watching
waiting . . .
  he
    stalks
      a tall
        gazelle
          deliberately
            masterfully
             he
          creeps
         along
        shh!
      and now . . .
      the jaws
        clamp
          down . . .

Christine Mathers (16)
North Leamington School

APPLE EXPERIENCE

The silence is unimaginable,
yet the noise is overwhelming.
The darkness of the bruises on the pale surface
give an insight into the life it started.
The loud crack of the stems when they break,
pounding on the hard ground like drums
    playing in the air.
Cold and damp, sweet and sour.
It bites when bitten, yet gives much pleasure.
A sphere of life, not unlike the world.
Flesh and juice, land and sea.
The core where it all began holds it in place,
    waiting.

The shape changes when sliced by a knife.
Two halves, which combined as one -
    the inside now visible.
Secrets now exposed for all to see.
One half removed, the bond is broken,
    the crunching is torture.
The second half begins to wilt.
A pale-brown creeps up around the edges
enveloping the flesh in a dark cloud.
The once pale-green skin is now a stained
    brown.
Wrinkles appear and deterioration
    begins to set in.
In no time the green, firm, solid sphere of life
    is
a dark, soft shape of death.

Kirsty Mansfield (16)
North Leamington School

The Castle

From the outside of the castle you can see a thorny jungle of briars
climbing right up to the top of the dark, high walls.
You can feel the mud squelching beneath your feet like gnarled
hands as you get nearer and nearer to the gloomy castle.
As you step inside the doorway, you are blinded by the cobwebs and
can't hear anything apart from the wind whistling behind you.
You walk further and further into the castle, then *'bang'* the door
is shut, you are all alone.
You feel a shiver go through your body as you walk down the
winding staircase.
You come to a cellar, as black as night, you feel like someone is
watching you with empty eyes, you run and run until you get back
to the old wooden door.
A growl of thunder startles you, then a streak of forked lightning.
Now that you've left, the castle is deserted.

Lisa Whittleton (11)
North Leamington School

My Head

Inside my head is a wonderful land,
where trees and fruit grow all year round.

On top of my head is a lush sea of brown hair,
I wouldn't want to swim in there!

Around my head is a harsh, cruel world,
where people fight all day and all night.

Beside my head are my friends and family,
not to mention my great, great granny!

Emma Thompson (11)
North Leamington School

Utopia

Show me where there is no pain or sadness,
Where I may sleep and ease my mind of care.
Where minds shall not be forced into madness,
By acts or deeds that they may witness there.
And on the faces of all people joy,
Sadness will not there enter hearts of men,
And war will not take either man or boy
From home or from the people who love them.
No desire will there be for ought than peace,
No will to torture or to maim or kill.
The hunger and starvation there will cease,
For crops will grow and men will eat their fill.
But is this land somewhere that I may find?
It's just a dream arising from men's minds.

Lucy Griffin (16)
North Leamington School

The Castle

The castle sat there, glistening in the rain whipped air.
'Must we walk through the thorny jungle?'
she said icily, hitching up her skirt.
They went down into the coal-black cellar darkness,
where there sat a little bow-legged dwarf.
His gnarled hands pointed at her, 'Who she?'
Then suddenly there was a tremendous clap of lightning.
It struck the castle and she was buried.
No one knew who she was or where she was in the gloomy,
spooky castle.

Rebekah Pink (11)
North Leamington School

The Castle

The old cart bumped along over the tree trunks
which pushed through the mud like gnarled hands.
The rain whipped and splashed with fierce rain drops,
as the lightning flashed through the trees.
The next streak of forked lightning lit up the ghastly castle
A thorny jungle grew up with greedy claws over the walls,
The collapsed roof suddenly looked like broken ribs,
Windows looked like empty eyes as the castle glared.
Thin slivers of broken glass shone in the windows.
Inside, thin grey draperies with crawling spiders covered the walls,
Bats fluttered as vampires in the cellar darkness.
Trees were swaying grotesquely.
The castle still rose up in the glistening wet.

Jackie Perry (11)
North Leamington School

The Castle

The castle roof is like cracked ribs,
Outside the rain whipped,
The walls of the castle glistening wet out of the darkness,
Streams of light hit the castle wall through the
jungle of briars,
The mud like gnarled hands,
Fierce raindrops bouncing off the floor,
The lightning flashes lighting up the sky,
Inside cobwebs on every wall,
Who would want to live here? Not me.

Matthew Harris (11)
North Leamington School

ANGER!

Anger is red
It smells like wood burning
And tastes like burnt toast
It looks like fire on a dark sky
And sounds like thunder and fireworks
Anger feels like a burning sun.

Harriet Whitehead (11)
North Leamington School

LOVE

Love is the shape of a heart,
With it beating fast.
Red and pink stripes are the colours.
It leads you into happiness.
Your heart is content with what you feel.
This is the life of love.

Sasha-Marie Chapman (12)
North Leamington School

MOODY SEA

M oaning, groaning, all day long,
O penly singing her unhappy song.
O nto the rocks, she crashes all day,
D oing her best to get her anger away.
Y esterday, she did nothing but moan,

S ome of the day, we've only heard groans.
E very day she ends up weeping,
A nd after that, she calms down, sleeping.

Lizzie Beresford (13)
Rugby High School

THE FUTURE

A vision of distortion,
A road I had laid,
But life made a loser in the game I had played.

Tomorrow came,
Tomorrow passed,
A shadow of me was no longer cast.

Take my advice,
Follow the rule,
Life can be fair, it need not be cruel.

The future is fate,
The past can be broken,
The words I speak now will remain unspoken.

Victoria Yeats (16)
Rugby High School

TIME

Time is the future, time is the past,
Time can be slow, time can be fast.
There is a time to do right and a time to be the best,
There is a time to work and a time to rest.
There's a time to feel sad and a time to feel great,
A time to love and a time to hate.
Time will not stop for you, or for me;
Time will not leave, it goes on endlessly.
Time is the future, time is the past,
Time is special so make sure it lasts.

Angharad Rees-Jones (15)
Rugby High School

POEM FOR AN ENGLISH TEACHER

Trickling, tumbling, tripping
Over stones, gambolling down hills,
Happy go lucky, filled with laughter,
Hurtling precariously round bends,
No cares, no worries, no responsibilities,
All around regal trees with kindly forbearance,
Look upon this madness and shake their laden branches
And the leaves repeat the message,
Whispering, rustling, wise,
'The river is young' they say
'Let it have its fun, let it play'
And the river hurtles on,
Nowhere to go, nowhere to be,
Not knowing why it must rush to who knows where,
But carrying on with unleashed gaiety,
Time passes, and with time grows knowledge
Nothing can be free forever,
Suddenly the river met the sea,
Calm, yet with a fiery temper
A guardian of vast secrets and infinite knowledge
Which it could choose to disclose at its own discretion,
The river did not want to be ruled by the sea
And tried to fight,
With one great wave the vast ocean silenced the tiny river
And said, 'Do you not think that you can learn from me?'
And then, although the river was not always good,
Often longing to be free,
It understood that everything changes and nothing lasts forever,
And with that understanding the river took its place in the sea.

Jenna Curtis (17)
Rugby High School

IN A MATCHBOX OF MY OWN

In a matchbox, where I spend my days,
Ducks swim happily in smouldering tar.
There is my windmill where the elephants lie,
Sleeping upon underfed beams of wood.

The gorillas are my soul companions,
For they lead no life of pain.
Their skin reflects all thoughts of evil,
Whilst resting their heads on pillows of harsh plastic.

Elephants awaken to greet the hot morning,
Ducks step out of their pond of tar.
Gorillas remain sleeping in their land of angels,
And the corners of the matchbox begin to disappear.

The days become endless,
Gorillas scream from inflamed trees,
Whilst the elephants stamp on burning ducks,
And the matchbox is gradually destroyed with rage.

Vikki Stone (15)
Rugby High School

I KNOW YOU?

Souls like shuttered windows,
Happiness yet not enough,
Peace that lost its way,
In this mind a lone dove.

Ideas prematurely born,
Fantasies died too young,
An early grave awaits us,
Yet am I the only one?

Piece by piece we notice,
Yet realise far too late,
What had I known before,
Replaced by inhuman hate.

Now and then I remember,
A hand lifts the lacy shroud,
What I see here before me:
A mirror in the crowd.

Amina Malik (16)
Rugby High School

KRISTAL NACHKT

Darkness clouds over, spreading its wings
Suffocating,
Overbearing,
Wrapping the world in a cocoon of fear.
Slowly, steadily, sparsely the hands turn
Second by second,
One by one.
Arms spread open and capture time
In control, out of control,
Which way, that way,
Crashing,
Smashing,
Broken crystal. Then
    Deadly silence.
Time failed to have any significance as souls became
lost.
Stars sparkled casting an eerie sense of desolation.
Lights blazed, the aftermath of a destructive scream of fire
and the rest of the world slept on, regardless,
safe in their warm cloak of ignorance.

Itohan Ugiagbe (15)
Rugby High School

FROZEN MOMENTS

Crackling cold and crooked
And scathing in her voice,
Like she's scratching at my skin.
Her eyes are black holes
Swallowing me up:
She has shares in gravity.
Then her fingers are tapping,
And her nails are hollow. Tapping
Alongside the second hand of the clock,
In and out of the seconds,
Dancing with them; racing them;
Cheating them, with hollow nails.
And now she's smiling, cold and crooked,
Smiling and tapping, at the clock,
With the seconds. Hollow seconds.
And she's speaking now. Right now.
Right this second because I can hear her -
Hear her voice like she's scratching at
My skin and tapping in my mind,
In between the seconds, in those
Lost instances not existing or
Belonging but intangible to time.
But she smiles on, laughs on, right now,
Cackling cold and empty in my head;
Hollow tapping, like she's scratching in my mind,
At my life. Dry and senseless smiles and words, yes:
She's speaking now, as if she has the right:
'Died,' is what she says: 'Died,' with hollow meaning
And incessant tapping which coldly wakes me
Every night in the empty seconds, old and crooked,
Crackling, scathing, scratching, cheating seconds
That don't exist, are void and dead, like they were yesterday.

Lucy Pogson (16)
Rugby High School

Now

In the beginning:
Nothing interrupts the vast expanse of grass -
Each blade selfishly intent on survival,
Except the odd defiant flower.
A sudden deluge of rain
Relentlessly, persistently, cruelly
Abuses its recipients on the ground,
Even the strongest
Weaken under the weight of the rain.

One thousand years later:
A tree has erupted
In unquestionably autumnal splendour,
Its glory undeniable.
A single leaf detaches itself from the body,
Unrestricted, it attempts to resist
The security radiating from the ground
And lingers in the air,
Before succumbing to the sod.

One thousand years later:
Winter now,
And a young boy walks gloved hand
In gloved hand with an old man
Down an otherwise dormant
Street lined with houses.
Their tenuous existence
Does not feel
Threatened
Because
To them
This is
Now.

Emily Reid (16)
Rugby High School

THE GLASS TEAR

Through the glass tear I see the pain of others.
The smell of sewage and bodies fill my nose.
Still the glass tear does not break.
The silent cries of men fill my ears
And the horror music of guns and bombs.
Still the glass tear does not break.
The sight of mudded trenches and blooded men.
The taste of decaying food and Ersatz coffee.
Still the glass tear does not break.
An *explosion* of guns and bombs.
The glass tear shatters into a thousand pieces.
I see the glorious red shine through,
A field of silent poppies.

Emma Jeffs (16)
Rugby High School

WHAT IS LIFE WITHOUT TIME?

Time itself is a miraculous thing,
Time is very much a living thing.
However hard you try, you can't escape from its clutches,
Its mighty, powerful, everlasting clutches.
Every minute that passes, is never to be seen again,
Lost in eternity, never to return again.
Time's closest and oldest companion is the clock,
The never ending ticking of the clock.
Time is permanent, untouchable, invincible to mankind,
And it has the potency to control mankind.
What is life without time?
This constant, dominating, indestructible time.

Jasdeep Toor (15)
Rugby High School

MATURITY OF BEING MATURE

It has to be kept secret,
Nobody is allowed to know,
Girls whisper and giggle,
Rumours begin.

Tell me, did you see him? Ooh when?
Well, he waved at me.
Let's follow him down the corridor.
Teenage stalkers.

The maturity of being immature,
It's part of being adolescent,
The immaturity if being mature.

In lessons twenty girls stare at
The blackboard, doodling hearts.
Playing the scene of him in their heads.

Twenty girls, head resting on hands,
Staring at the blackboard, silent and still,
Their hearts racing.

He's in the next classroom,
The bell, a race, as twenty
Faces fight to peer through a patch of glass.

He brushes against someone's arm.
The group swoon.
The girl refuses to wash.

It's part of being adolescent,
The maturity of being immature,
The immaturity of being mature.

Rebekah Greenslade (16)
Rugby High School

BEAUTY (A MALE PERSPECTIVE)

It was a great day when I met her, the sun hung in the sky.
She looked like an angel from heaven, where men may go to die.
The images of her walking slowly through the field
Gave me the images of roses, she was a beautiful yield.

Her face was painted with the innocence of newborn foals,
Her figure was beauty complete, she was a diamond among coals.

When I first met her my heart burst through the cage that it was kept in.
My eyes sprung wide open, I literally leapt.
Was she for real? I had to be sure.
This phenomenal creature had no visible flaw.

Now I'll tell you a fact that is perfectly true.
I would cease to exist if I had to go on without you.
Where you walk, angels sing;
I love you more, than anything.

Suzanne Gilkes (16)
Rugby High School

THE VIOLENT SEA

The wind whipped cunningly around the cliffs that day.
Violent waves crashed menacingly against the shore,
Embracing the sand back to its dismal lair,
Ejecting it like a vile burden,
Throwing it onto the sand.
The white foam interlacing itself between the gritty grains,
The wind grew calm,
Waves reduced to rhythmical ripples,
Waterlogged sand seeping out of the crevices.
Seaweed laid stranded and entwined across the rocks,
All was calm.

Lisa Dale (15)
Rugby High School

SO LITTLE TIME, SO UNAWARE

The proud liner, full of life,
Sailing across the ocean,
A vast space, an empty space,
Surrounded by calmness and peace.
But so little time and so unaware of the events to come.

Confidence, beauty, pride,
None lacking in this ship.
The ocean so still, never ending,
A blanket of water, harmless, innocent, deceiving.
But so little time, so unaware of the disaster yet to come.

The lonely sea, a fooling emptiness,
So silent and tranquil.
But it is there in the distance,
Like a dagger cutting through the smoothness of the blanket,
Destroying the continuity, cold and harsh,
So little time, so unaware of the consequences.

Then it comes out of the darkness,
Like an electric shock, lethal and deadly.
'Iceberg ahead!' but it is too late.
Panic! Fear! Danger!
The ship breaks, disappearing under the blanket.
Piercing screams, pain, confusion,
So little time and so unaware that death is ahead. Titanic is doomed.

Sahra Ali (16)
Rugby High School

DEEP-PRESSING

Confined within her soul
Going deeper, getting darker
Deeper still
Feel the pressure
Intense pressure
Pressure exists within the depths
The depths of her soul
Relationships discovered
Pressure unearthed
Environment uncovered
Pressure unearthed
Searching the depths
A bottomless soul
No escape
No way out
Imprisoned in the depths
Of a hostile soul
Deep-pressing
Alone.

Louise Leighton (15)
Rugby High School

LOST MEMORIES

The ocean is where
My memories lie
Down in the darkness
Lost in another time

But they're drifting away
Out of my reach
If only I could spread my hands
To catch another glimpse

Of that other world
Where my happiness lies
To forget the sorrow
And the sadness of my eyes

The ocean is where
My memories lie
It's another world
Lost in another time.

Gela Veshagh (15)
Rugby High School

THE TIME MINE

Far away from here
In a distant dimension
Time sits quietly

Each gleaming pearl drop
Shimmering gems; moments of
Our lives to be lived

In caves they lie still
Waiting for their destiny
Light against the dark

Now, one floats away
Drifts into oblivion
Moments lived and gone

And so they go on
Until the angel straddles
The earth and cries out

Time no longer!

Juliette Harrisson (15)
Rugby High School

WHO FIRED THE GUN AT THE START?

Who first decided that today would be today?
That we started counting, and waiting,
And watching, for the clouds to speed across the sky,
With hopes so high that our breath was bated,
Who said, 'Too late! That was yesterday.'

Who decided on the sixty minutes for each passing hour?
That we await with such anticipation,
That is won by each second we dream,
With our hopes carried high in our hands,
Who reaches for the immense shift of power?

Who dictated the waiting and the wanting?
The loss we feel after each moment is past,
The tears we shed for memories lost, forever,
With chances we had, falling just out of reach,
Who dictated the eternal yearning?

Joanne Konkel (15)
Rugby High School

THE DREAM

The dream is flowing
Flowing over me - filling me
Its pale, jade textures are touching me
Tempting me, softening me
Rubbing me, creating warmth
I feel alive!

The dream is kicking
Kicking through me - shaking me
Its bright red textures are chasing me
Pushing me, shouting at me
Fighting for me, striking cold
I feel inspired!

The dream is running
Stunning every part of me - lifting me
Its quiet, strong textures are loving me
Wanting me, wounding me
Forming me, protecting me
I feel on fire!

Irene White (18)
Rugby High School

THE HEATHER

The whispering heather ripples in the breeze,
Before lulling itself into silent anticipation.
A haggard traveller stumbles through its midst.
Seating himself on a small outcrop, he waits.
A fiery sphere slips out of the purple sky
To fall noiselessly behind a distant hill.
He takes out a battered harmonica,
And putting it clumsily to his cracked lips,
He plays a tune he can no longer remember.
By this time, a swift gliding ivory pearl
Has nestled itself amongst the fluffy clouds.
The traveller lays himself on the ground
To gaze at the diamonds sparkling above.
He swigs whisky from his battered hip-flask,
Thinking of the happiness he once knew.

As soon as the dawn spreads itself across the moors,
Shattering the darkness into nothing.
He gathers his things and stumbles on his way;
He feels out of place among such beauty.
The heather is silent for a moment longer
Then resumes its eternal whispering.

Cara Bemrose (17)
Rugby High School

The Beach

As I walked down the lonely beach,
I was not alone,
There were three people within my reach,
Splashing through the foam.

As we splashed through the shallow waves,
The three of them and me,
I cannot think of happier days,
Than splashing through the sea.

The North Sea is so icy cold,
Even in the month of May,
But my family and I are so bold,
And walk throughout the day.

When I return to the lonely beach,
I won't be alone,
There will be three people within my reach,
Splashing through the foam.

Charlotte Parkins (15)
Rugby High School

Him

He wants more than you can give,
His life depends on you,
He needs your help so he can live,
But what are you to do?

He loves you more than words can say,
But he can't carry on,
Without your help he'll fade away,
His soul will soon be gone.

So will you stay and help your friend,
Or will you leave his life?
If you leave the guilt won't end,
And if you stay you'll end his strife.

He's coming back, he's trusting you,
Keep the love alive,
Hold him tight and love him too,
Be there so he'll survive.

Lynsey Smith (15)
Rugby High School

STANDARD FORM

As time goes on
It occurs to me,
That life isn't exactly
As it's meant to be.
With no sign of two parents,
Two children and a cat,
What am I?
A phenomenon?
No, not that.
Happy families are no longer the 'norm',
Doesn't matter if you're not 'standard form'.
Who wants the warmth, the happiness, the bickering . . .
Do you?
That's all a big family does.
I prefer two.

Claire Gladwin (15)
Rugby High School

LOST

I sat up yesterday,
I looked all around,
There was no one there,
I realised then,
I was not alone,
But lost.

I was warm,
But cold,
Lost in confusion,
As I shivered,
I was afraid,
But not alone,
I was lost.

Isolated in a world of terror,
Company for my thoughts,
My only friend,
No friends,
With my vision,
I was lost.

Kate Dunlop (15)
Rugby High School

TIME WAITS FOR NO ONE

Time waits for no one,
Or so, someone once said.
But somehow I haven't been able
To get the idea out of my head.

What if time stood still
At the chiming of a clock?
Would our neighbours keep on arguing,
Heard all over the block?

Time doesn't wait for me,
I have to keep striving on.
I'll probably still be racing time
Even when I'm gone.

Time waits for no one,
Or so, someone once said.
But time waits for some,
For those who are dead.

Ria Smulovic (16)
Rugby High School

THE MYSTERIES OF A GARDEN

Gushes, gushing of cool air through
Trees, trees scattering wildly the
Leaves, leaves that are brown, crispy and
Yellow, yellow like the
Sun, blasting its bolts of roaring
Fire, fire burning the leaves into ashes
and
Smoke, smelling strong in the hot air.

Laughter, small children laughing
whilst
Playing, playing with their tricycles and
Balls, full of air, bouncing up and
Down. Down the rain pours
Whistling, whistles as it spins to the
Ground, the ground wet with pools of
water.
The wind, gentle and soothing,
Or tyrannous full of turmoil and anger.

Claire Gulliver (15)
Rugby High School

A Whisper

You have a secret . . . a desire,
      a lover?
You whisper . . . and now the secret's no longer.
Your lover . . . a squire,
      a courtier,
      a suitor.
Your suitor . . .
      your squire,
      your secret, no longer.
A courtier . . . a suitor,
      a lover,
      your squire.
A secret delivered . . . to your courtier,
By your whisper . . . from your lover.

Natalie Hoath (13)
Rugby High School

Satisfaction

Why do we persecute people further
When we have already torn them limb from limb?
And why when we have finally destroyed them
Do we not rest until we have scattered their ashes?
And even then we are not content
Until we have seen the wind
Pick them up
And carry them away.
But even their destruction does not gratify
And our conscience desperately screams for satisfaction.
But remorse and regret
Is all that is left
To comfort the black heart of the destroyer.

Hannah Griffiths (14)
Rugby High School

THE NIGHT OF MOURNING

He knows there is nothing more he can do tonight,
As he watches her helplessly, giving up the fight.
He closes his eyes and stands aside,
Now only God can be her guide.

A sharp breath in,
The tears begin to form.
He touches her face,
She is no longer warm.

He remembers how it used to be,
All the happy times they shared,
Out of all the people,
They had been paired.

Now it is here,
The time has arrived,
His one and only
True love has died.

Lucy Ogburn (15)
Rugby High School

THE RAINBOW

The spectrum gleams in heaven up high
Multicolours catching my eyes
I turn to face towards the glow
I feel the rain, but the sunshine's so
The rainbow like a huge drawbridge
Spreading the colour from ridge to ridge
Where the rainbow ends I cannot see
A pot of gold awaits for me.

Kirsty Lewis (11)
Rugby High School

YOUNGSTERS OF POVERTY

No one cares if they live or die.
Ashamed feelings are hidden away.
They are deprived of life,
By an unjust world.
Only they know the wickedness they're held in.
They struggle,
But fail.
They are trapped somewhere where many will never arrive.
The fear, the hatred, the misery,
A smile very seldom seen.
Why, why?
What is it like for them?
We can't imagine.
How can we?
The pain
Forever. Never forgotten.

Emma Alsop (15)
Rugby High School

THE SEA

A patchwork of rainbow coloured coral.
A multitude of quicksilver, flitting fish.
A shoal of delicate, glass bubbles.
A stream of delving, golden light.
A congregation of iridescent, shimmering mermaids.
An assembly of frolicsome, frisky dolphins.

A flock of feathered, flightsome seagulls.
A fleet of shining, billowing sails.
A cloud of short, stout puffins.
A mingle of summer coloured boats.
A wave of fluorescent, plastic dinghies.
A parade of milky, frothed foam.

A giggle of sun-warmed, rosy children.
A worry of anxious, frustrated mothers.
A group of sandy, soaked fathers.
A row of shiny, bright buckets.
A line of slippery, slimy seaweed.
A swirl of pastel, textured shells.

Hannah Davies (12)
Rugby High School

KNOW LIFE

You have to cling on and let go,
To be silent and speak out,
You should know how to feel,
And know how to deal,
With what has gone by and what is to come,
To you.

You have to learn to cope and keep calm,
To get on with your life,
To know what to do,
When everything's wrong,
And nothing seems to go right,
For you.

You have to remember to laugh,
To have fun and to play,
But to know when to stop,
When to cry and to weep,
When to remember the memories,
You've had.

To understand what you've got,
To keep it forever, you've had, for you, to you,
Is precious.

Holly Inman (15)
Rugby High School

BUSY LINES

Somewhere faraway the phone rings,
Bring-ring, bring-ring (it's swiftly answered).
'Two large margarita pizzas with extra cheese, please.'
'Thank you, sir' - the phone rings with the next order.

Somewhere faraway the phone rings,
Bring-ring, bring-ring (it's held for a while).
'Please hold for one moment, all lines are engaged.'
'Oh blast! I'm paying for this' - Greensleeves fills the line.

Somewhere faraway the phone rings,
Bring-ring, bring-ring (the answerphone is activated).
'Um, hello Mum. How are you? Ring me when you can.'
An old lady lies unconscious - the lifeline out of reach.

Somewhere faraway the phone rings,
Bring-ring, bring-ring (it's picked up).
'Can I interest you in double glazing, madam?'
'No thank you' - the phone is slammed down.

Somewhere faraway the phone rings,
Bring-ring, bring-ring (it's nervously lifted).
'Hi Anna, fancy coming out with me tonight?'
'Oh yes Gary' - the phone line buzzes on for hours.

Meriel Close (15)
Rugby High School

I Wonder...

I wonder what the forest would be like
With no trees to hide behind,
No rocks for ants to crawl under,
And no flowers to blossom.

I wonder what the country would look like
With no animals to graze there,
No vegetation to grow there,
And no sun to shine.

I wonder what the playground would sound like
With no noisy children,
No bell to ring,
And no games to play.

I wonder what the air would smell like
With no aroma to fill it,
No freshener to spray in it,
And no pollution in it.

I wonder what the world would be like
Without my life as part of it;
But then
I wouldn't be able to wonder.

Sarah Hughes (14)
Rugby High School

I Wonder . . .

I wonder what would happen,
if an idiot was in charge,
of all the nuclear warheads,
throughout the world at large.

If the director of the NHS,
died of a heart attack,
would the doctor who tried to save him,
almost definitely get the sack?

I wonder what would happen,
if a meteorite hit earth.
Do you think that time would contract,
to the moment of my birth?

If throughout the human race,
infertility did spread,
would we find a cure,
or would we all end up dead?

I wonder what will happen,
when the world's energy sources run out,
and when the ice caps melt,
and all there is, is water about.

I wonder, I wonder,
what would happen and what will,
I wonder too much,
or at least I think I do.

Charlie Winn (15)
Rugby High School

So Close

I could have been on that bus,
Or walked through your street,
Ate in that restaurant.
But I didn't.

Or I did, but not at the right time.
You got off a stop before I got on,
I took a diversion,
And never made it to your street -
Except just past the corner,
Two minutes before you dropped your shopping there.

And the food at the café was great - wasn't it?
But my budget wasn't.
So I left after one drink -
And opted for the chippy.

And I walked home - lonely,
And you drove home - lonely.

But you stop at the traffic lights,
Just as I cross.
You seem familiar -
So often we've nearly met.
And we smile like old friends -
'Hop in' you say, 'we've wasted time!'

Amelia Lee (16)
Rugby High School

A Forgotten War

Endless nights
Down in the shelter.
The cold night bites,
Sending shivers down my spine.

Count 1 to 10.
Wait in suspense.
Thank the Lord, it missed us again.
But it hit someone else.

Thousands dead.
Millions homeless.
Why not peace instead?
Why are we sentenced to war?

Lucy Keay (14)
Rugby High School

Amidst The Ocean

The water's calm, a subtle blue,
A creation once so unique and new.
Lays ridden upon our gracious land
And washes upon each grain of sand.

What wonders lay beneath the shore?
Such extraordinary creatures I am sure.
That wander the ocean so fresh and blue,
A privilege given from Him to you.

As I drift between two shores afar,
I glance above at the glimmering stars.
I care not as I begin to drift away
Ready to face another day.

Alicia Mistry (15)
Rugby High School

To My Best Friend

Dream days
Dance and vanish
Childhood dreams
Of candy-coated life
The sticky, sweet seconds
That lasted a lifetime
When we could do anything
Or be
Anything
And no one cared.
Touch a star
And bring one back for me
My friend
Till life comes down
And pulls away the blankets
That shelter
And it's cold outside
And so I have to say goodbye
Too soon
Don't cry
Because if I have to go away
Know I'll be back for you someday
And even though you're sad right now
I'm going to wipe away those tears somehow
So can't you hold on a little longer?
Try to be a little stronger?
And I'll come to hold your hand
I know you understand
And we'll always be
Best friends.

Jasmine Reynolds (16)
Rugby High School

FREEDOM

I hear the sounds in my head,
Clearly, all so clearly.
The thought of all those people dead
It scared me, oh it scared me.
The screams I heard all through the night
Made me wish for broad daylight,
It scared me, oh it scared me.

The smell of that big killing camp,
I will never forget it.
The smell of death, the smell of fright
It scared me, oh it scared me.
The thought 'It is nearly my turn'
Made my insides curl and burn.
I lived off the dream that 'Maybe not.'
It relieved me, it relieved me.

Then one day the big time came,
I was overjoyed, yes overjoyed.
Those big tall gates that were very wide,
Slowly moved into the sides,
Letting in fresh air,
It relieved me, it relieved me.
No one moving, no one breathing,
The only sound was someone sneezing.
I was happy, yes I was happy.

The final day, the coming out,
Made me want to shout right out.
The happiness of breathing in
Fresh air and hearing birds.
The joy of seeing those for whom I care.
The memories just bad times in the past.
I have my freedom now, at last.

Tania Hayes (16)
Rugby High School

One Chance

Time will not stop and wait for anyone,
There is no *time* for regrets,
The *past* cannot be altered,
The *future* brings new opportunities,
The *present* is for living,
Life is precious and can never be repeated,
Why waste a *gift*,
That is so *invaluable* and one that so many take for granted
And others do *not*
Live *life* to the full -
There is only *one* chance . . .

Sarah Peck (15)
Rugby High School

Just A Butterfly!

Floating, gliding, falling, diving
Dipping and darting, dancing on air.
Skimming and swirling, swooping,
Yet silent.
Soft as a feather,
Breathless beauty.
Blazing with brightness
Colourful collage of crimson, orange, purple and blue
Beautiful, beckoning, whispering wings, quietly fluttering
Out of my view.

Rebecca Kelly (11)
Rugby High School

BED WITH BROLLY

As I glanced at my watch,
It was clear to see,
When my mother looked at me,
'Twas time at last to go to bed,
She looked again 'By Jove' she said,
'Lexy Lay you are a wally,
There is no need to take a brolly,
It would be better with a dolly,
For with you to sleep,
It would be,
Yes,
More practical,
'Cause I'm sure the roof won't leak.'

But these wise old words had slipped my mind,
And in the morning I did find,
Plenty of bruises,
Occurred in my snoozes,
And it was clear to see,
The brolly's spokes,
With their pinches and pokes,
Had been attacking me.

Lexy Lay (15)
Rugby High School

Chair

'Pretend the chair is your mother'
The psychologist said.
So I did.
I'd like to say I took the wooden spoon
And beat its worn upholstery
Until the dust rose in a fury
And made the shape unclear
But I didn't
Instead I cried.
'Pretend the chair is your father'
Said the psychologist.
So I did.
I'd like to say I took the wooden spoon
And beat its floral falsification
Until the old cotton gave way
But I didn't
I remained quiet.
'Is there nothing you have to
Share with the chair?'
Asked the psychologist
'Have you no unfinished business
With the chair?'
Then, 'That chair is your parents'
I went over to the chair
And sat on it.
The chair looked after me.

Miriam Sturdee (16)
Rugby High School

Keer Zyn Vorloren Geust - Time Gone Astray

It is the start, the dawn of time,
An innocent world, no thought of crime.
First came love, and followed hate,
And then for peace, it was too late.
Women wept, and children cried,
As in war, their men folk died.
'Give us justice! Avenge the dead!
We want revenge!' the people said.

It is the end, all justice done,
No evil left, all battles won.
A perfect world, nothing is wrong,
No children's chatter, no bird song.
Justice was served, no sinning let,
When evil was, with evil met.
One thing though, will save us yet,
If we forgive and we forget.

Margaret Bennett (15)
Rugby High School

Elephant

Big, soft eyes gaze sadly
Ears like leathery sails blow wide
A small calf hides between the towering tree trunks of her legs
And feels the pulse beat through her wrinkled hide.

Protectively, she guards her child
Carried inside her for two years
Gently, their trunks entwined together young and old
She shields it from her fears.

Wrinkles show her wisdom
Behind each ear is desert sand
Her tusks shine ivory, these trophies of her life
Only an elephant could understand.

And when she is gone
Any elephant that nears
Will see the tusks, her trophies of life
And softly weep
Elephant tears.

Katy Cross (13)
Rugby High School

I WISH...

I wish I lived in the country,
Instead of this busy city,
Where instead of grass it's towers.

I wish I could see the stars at night,
Instead of the polluted sky,
That hangs above my head.

I wish I could go out at night,
Without the thoughts of what lurks,
In the dark and dingy alleyways.

I wish I could smell the country aroma,
Instead of the polluted air,
I smell out of my window.

I wish I could go to sleep at night,
Without hearing the couple
Shouting above my head.

Debbie Holmes (14)
Rugby High School

STAGES OF THE SEA

On peaceful days,
The sea is a beautiful choir,
Chanting rhythmically,
The rocks knocking together,
They are the pulse,
Of the never-ending tune.

When the sea becomes a raging crowd,
Fighting for some unknown prize,
The sea is no longer a choir,
It is a group of people!
Angry at some evil
Fighting against the cliff face walls,
As if some barricade is holding them back.

When I'm lying on the beach,
Listening to the waves,
In my mind they're beckoning,
Trying to attract me to the underwater world.

Some people say the sea is an animal,
A he or a she,
But to me the sea is a sea,
It is original, unique.
There is only one type,
There is only one name,
It's the sea!

Samantha Butterworth (12)
Rugby High School

THE SEA!

Magnificent, wondrous, deadly, calm,
        The sea.

It sputters, wondering what to do next,
It sprays water, hissing at life,
The clouds are angry.
They bang together and . . .
Flash!
Lightning.
Bang!
Thunder.
The sea roaring madly at the dripping tears.
It screams, it moans, the ship goes down.
Fire striking wood.
Dead corpses float around.
Reality strikes.
They sink.
They sink to their watery deaths.

The sea just moves calmly now.
Silently, victoriously.
It has won the war -
The war to stay alive.

Magnificent, wondrous, deadly, calm,
        The sea.

Hannah Edwards (12)
Rugby High School

TIGER

Deep in the long grass, I hide,
Staring at the distant horizon.
The sun is setting,
And the world is covered with a thick, black sheet.

My eyes gleam in the starlight,
I creep forward, slowly emerging.
A collage of orange and gold,
Covered from head to tail with black stripes.
I'm unique, I'm like no other.
Snowy-white whiskers, pink rasping tongue, emerald green eyes
- No one else is like me.

Ahead, a buffalo is drinking,
Not even realising I'm there . . . it's mealtime.
Creeping, not daring to breathe,
Low and slow, then I charge.
Chasing it and chasing it, until I spring,
Thrusting my teeth into its neck - dead.

Back to my hiding, dragging it with my claws.
Striding through the long grass.
I feast in the moonlight,
Then rest, waiting for dawn to come.
Satisfied . . . until next time.

Hayley Eames (12)
Rugby High School

WHALES

Unsuspecting, calm and peaceful,
Gliding graceful through the sea,
The blue, the never ending blue,
Deep as deep can be.

Unsuspecting, calm and peaceful,
Gliding graceful through the sea,
Whalers waiting ready to pounce,
Harpoons loaded - ready, aim, *fire!*

Unsuspecting, calm and peaceful,
Gliding graceful through the sea,
The treacherous *boom* of the killing machine,
Man strikes again.

Unsuspecting, calm and peaceful,
Gliding graceful through the sea,
See the whale so big and heavy,
Helpless, useless, dead.

Unsuspecting, calm and peaceful,
Gliding graceful through the sea,
The red, the never ending red,
Deep as deep can be.

Emily-Jane Arbon (12)
Rugby High School

THE SEA

The raging wind generates,
Raging, ragged curls,
The crashing waves crush,
The jagged rocks below.

The clouds rumble down the mountain,
To guard it from the piercing wind,
And smashing waves,
The white wave crests blinking to the surface.

The clouds split into a porthole,
To let the sun ball through,
The glaring, storm-snaring sun
Snares the storm to a gentle breeze.

The waves stop to dive so deep,
And lap away at the shore,
Dragging down pearl pebbles and sand,
Back to drown below.

Jennifer Deeley (12)
Rugby High School

LEOPARD

The leopard lies in dappled light,
Waiting for its prey,
Soon she will take swift-footed flight,
Fly many miles away.

On balanced heels she bounds around,
Searching all the way,
In trees with food, she can be found,
Satisfying hunger with her prey.

But life is dangerous always,
For these precious cats,
For on certain terrible days,
Hunters plant snares and traps.

Their beautiful coats are in high demand,
For the fashion show,
So the hunters comb the desolate land,
Like seeds, their traps they sow.

Sara Balsom (12)
Rugby High School

THE FIRST DAY AT A NEW SCHOOL

I fell from a cloud from which I was on top
Hurtling towards the ground
A single, solitary raindrop
Falling in one quick journey from the top to the bottom.

I touched the ground, all on my own
Waiting
All alone. Isolated, lonely and lost
My friends fell and left me.

I dripped and spread over the ground
More raindrops fell
I formed a group of friends, a puddle
And I spread
Transformed into a pond, a stream, a river, a lake.

I felt joined I knew someone
A term went by
Now I am an ocean.

Emilie Day (12)
Rugby High School

AUTUMN

Autumn
With leaves falling swiftly from the trees,
A shower of colour.
Autumn
Trees become bare,
Plants begin to die.
Autumn
Early morning cobwebs covered with dew,
As water vapour appears.
Autumn
Animals hibernating,
Sleeping, wrapped up away from the cold.
Autumn
The cold weather starts to come,
Children are no longer seen after school.
Autumn
Children get excited,
Soon Santa will come.
Autumn
Winter is on its way,
Surprises are sure to happen.

Shelley Holland (11)
Rugby High School

NATURE

I wake up in the morning
the sunshine streaming in.
The sweet smell of flowers
just wanting me to begin.

I go out into the garden
the birds sing all around.
The sweet crunch of leaves
as my foot grasps the ground.

The redeeming smell of primrose
as I walk about the country.
The animals jump excitedly
just waiting for my company.

I start to walk home
looking forward to the night.
I snuggle up in my quilt
the sunset is just so bright.

Isabelle Jeffery (13)
Rugby High School

IT'S THE NOT KNOWING . . .

Massacre and murder
Bleakness and dark
Disaster and devastation
But in the end
It's the not knowing . . .

Dead or alive
Tortured or peaceful
Near or far away
But in the end
It's just the not knowing . . .

Heartless and cruel
World versus Nazis
Good against evil
But in the end
It's simply just the not knowing . . .

And that's what kills the hope in all of us . . .

Lucy Faulkner (13)
Rugby High School

EXCUSES

I've written the wrong name Miss,
There's paper in my eye,
I've swallowed an ink cartridge Miss,
I think I'm going to die!

I've smashed all the lights Miss,
I'm falling down a hole,
The school has been flooded Miss,
And I've broken the Egyptian bowl!

Who are those men with machine guns Miss?
Why are they pointing at me?
I think I'm about to be shot Miss,
And I've just been stung by a bee!

I've just pulled down the blinds Miss,
And they've just made a hole in my sock,
I don't feel very well Miss,
So please turn back the clock!

Amy Grewcock (12)
Rugby High School

TIME STOOD STILL

Time stood still for a moment
Silently contemplating beginning
Out of the dark, nothingness
Turned into the universe.

A great clear bang, and from the dark
An expanse was formed,
Shining brightly, infinitely radiant,
Empty, yet full to the brim.

Planets orbit around the bomb that is time,
Yet time is ticking away
The universe; waiting for the judgement day
When time will stand still again.

Sarah Glenn (15)
Rugby High School

UNDERWATER REALM

Teasing, taunting,
Almost there but not quite,
Its calm solidness,
Its smouldering waves,
The murdering blackness,
The life giving blue.

Huge sea elephants, massive and grey,
Down to the tiny sea horse, prancing in the emerald sea,
All alive in its murky depths,
Deep down,
Where no prying eyes can spy,
The magical underwater realm.

Where multicoloured princes glide around,
Their bright princesses following,
The mysterious octopus, clouded in inky darkness,
Seeing but not to be seen,
The quiet sleepy plaice,
Down at the bottom of the sea.

Up to the surface now, to the bright, bright world
Of the humans.

Hannah Bayliss (12)
Rugby High School

WINTER

Skaters skating on the lake
After eating Christmas cake
Winter

Ponds like glass reflect the past
Animals sleep on a winter fast
Winter

Harvest time has been and gone
Spring will not be very long
Winter

Icicles hanging from the frosted trees
The wind that blows like a restless sea
Winter

Robin redbreast standing on the garden fork
Looking for some scraps of Christmas pork
Winter

Santa Claus with his sack
Christmas presents waiting to be stacked
Winter

Winter is a happy time
The best time of year
You can eat some Christmas cake
And give Santa a cheer.

Stephanie Greer (11)
Rugby High School

LIGHTNING

Lightning in the sky
    bright, white light
        gone in a second
    crash, flash, boom
thunder joins in now
      then the shining returns.
        glimmering,
    shimmering in the sky.
gone.

Joanne Prior (14)
Rugby High School

WHAT I REALLY WANT

I absently brush a fly from my lips,
only for another to land on my eye.
The sun glares down on my back,
mercilessly penetrating my skin.
The bleak landscape shimmers in the
heat of the long afternoon.

I long for the crystal, sparkling water
to trickle down my parched throat
and cascade over me in beautiful rivulets.
For the glistening drops to soothe me enough
for my mind to think and my heart to love.
What I really want is life.

Daniel Bishop (12)
St Benedict's RC High School

LONELINESS

I look around, but all I see is
Emptiness.
A desolate place where nobody dares to go
I'm all alone -
Separated from all who care for me.
The void in my life is
still waiting to be fulfilled
Nobody cares!
The pain I feel goes unnoticed -
Nobody wants to know.
Loneliness -
The worst kind of depression.
Total isolation -
A desolate place where nobody dares to go.

Kathy McGreal (13)
St Benedict's RC High School

I MISS MY BEST FRIEND!

Alex was and still is my best friend,
He was the best friend I ever had,
I had lots of other friends too,
And I am making new friends,
He went to my school, I liked it there,
I like it here, I am settling in,
I played a lot of sport,
I got into mischief,
I miss my best friend,
I want to go home!

David Ryan (12)
St Benedict's RC High School

THE SCREEN

Darkness in the room
Light from the screen
Loud noises from all sides
Heart pumping, making you jump
Excitement from the movie
Eyes open wide
Taking in every 'mmm' of the screen
Great expectation
From the movie
Pleasure coming
From the atmosphere
Taste from the popcorn and pop
The sound of the muttering from the audience.

Matthew Torjussen (12)
St Benedict's RC High School

SEASONS

S nowing has finished.
P eering through, you see light,
R ays of sun coming through,
I   n the window,
N othing is wet,
G irls and boys are playing.

S un is at its hottest,
U sing the shade of a tree,
M orning's always bright,
M other's eyes blink at the sight,
E veryday it is sunny,
R ain stops and sun appears.

Andrew Roberts (11)
St Benedict's RC High School

Dark Water, Blue Mist

Waves are dancing, foaming, white horses,
Dark sky looming overhead,
Feel the power, the sea taking you,
Strength surging from surface to bed.

Water beating on the cliff side,
Distant ships rocking to and fro,
Bowing to the sea's cruel hunger
With sails a-bursting, flag a-blowing.

Over the howl of roaring tide,
A distant voice can be heard
As if at once the storm softened
Under the voices magic spell.

Sea's strength ebbed as if by magic,
Ferocious battle now seemed dead
Water cooled, calm and still,
'Storm in a teacup soon blow over!'

Georgie Bradley (11)
St Benedict's RC High School

Holidays

H aving fun at the beach,
O n fun trips to anywhere,
L ovely things to see and do,
I n a caravan, hotel or flat
D ays and days to play too,
A fter we go and dance away,
Y ou enjoy yourselves so very much . . .
S adly you have to go.

Jennifer Spires (12)
St Benedict's RC High School

FIRE!

I heard the screams,
I heard the shouts of fire,
There isn't a fire,
Someone's a liar.

Everyone is running,
Everyone is pushing,
It must be a joke,
There's no smoke.

People crying,
Grabbing possessions,
It's not very hot,
Someone's lost the plot!

Joanne Clarke (12)
St Benedict's RC High School

AUTUMN

I walk to school down the road,
My cheeks are rosy-red,
I slip then fall on the frost,
I wish I could go back to bed.

I'm halfway there, to school,
My fingers are icy-cold.
I feel like going straight back home,
But 'I mustn't be late' I was told.

Oh well! Here I am , it's great!
Well I feel better, I see my mate!

Genevieve Hughes (11)
St Benedict's RC High School

WE ALL GET LONELY SOMETIMES

There's an old man in his rocking chair
Sitting and smoking a pipe
With none of his family around him
We all get lonely sometimes.

A young man walks past
And laughs quietly to himself
'Stupid old man' he sniggers
'I'll never end up like that!'

The young man grew older,
Got married and had children.
But one by one they left him
And he began to feel alone.

He felt vulnerable, he felt empty
He felt his life was done
He thought he'd never been alone before
A long, long time ago.

Now *he's* the old man in the rocking chair
Who's sitting and smoking a pipe
With none of his family around him
He knew! We all get lonely sometimes.

Nicola Torrance (13)
St Benedict's RC High School

SUMMER AND AUTUMN

Summer is hopefully hot
but sometimes it is not.
Lying on the beach
with a big juicy peach.

Autumn starts to bring cold weather
I don't think I've seen a warm one, never
The leaves fall off the trees
like you wouldn't believe.
It's autumn my dear, oh dear!

Sara Andrews (11)
St Benedict's RC High School

WEATHER

W eather is fun
E arth is its target for the rain and sun.
A ll the time it changes.
T he weather is different everywhere.
H opefully today no one will moan about the weather.
E very day people complain about the weather.
R ain is the most constant of them all.

Christopher Whittingham (11)
St Benedict's RC High School

SOCCER

To walk out onto the pitch
with my brand new boots
awaiting my new challenge
I'm excited and nervous.

To compete against the best
it was easy to beat the rest.
Emotional when we lose
ace when we grab glory.
My muddy boots tell the best story.

Christopher Davies (11)
St Benedict's RC High School

BONFIRE NIGHT

The dark night sky interrupted
Spit! Crackle! Pop!
The bonfire is lit.
Bang! Crash! Sizzle!
The fireworks begin
Catherine Wheels turning
Rockets whirring
The flames roar
Orange, yellow, red
Lights are flying high above
Away flies the dove.

Anna Middleton (11)
St Benedict's RC High School

TEACHER TROUBLES

Every day I dread,
Teaching at this school,
The children are obnoxious,
And make me look a fool.

But sometimes, every now and then,
I think my God, it's not in vain,
All my work with ink and pen,
Has sunk in, to my little *'dears'* again.

Now it's the end of the day,
Hometime's my favourite by far,
When I get home I lay back and relax,
And tell myself I'm a star.

Laura Kerr (11)
Southam School

SCHOOL DINNERS

I walk into the canteen,
The smell of rotting cabbage,
Floats into my nose.

I walk into the line,
Where I am passed a plate,
I walk past the mouldy chicken.
Which is plopped onto my plate.

I walk on like a soldier,
On and on past the peas, which are,
Just like terrible grenades.

I walk up to the semolina,
All sloppy and revolting,
The cook gives me an evil grin,
She slops it into a bowl,
Passes it to me and says,
'Is that all my little pumpkin?'

Sophie Palmizi (11)
Southam School

SCHOOL

S port is good
C ool teachers
H ouse points
O dd teachers
O bservant teachers
L essons are good.

Oliver Longden (11)
Southam School

Poem About School

M aths is not fun.
A t all!
T wo times two is easy,
H omework once again
   Oh no!
S chool time again oh no!
   it's maths.

S chool is OK
C lasses are OK
H ometime is brilliant
O pen evening is bad,
   but
O nly sometimes, my mum
   goes.
L earning is sometimes
   OK . . .

Hayley Leahy (12)
Southam School

Vampire Poem

V ampires come out at night.
A stral shapes dancing in the sky.
M irrors I avoid I hate my face.
P sychic powers are in my grasp.
I mmoral fangs take a bite dealing
   are my delight.
R elishing rich-red blood.
E ctoplastic shapes envelop.
S upernatural, soul, spirit sleep all day
   and wake at night.

Vicky Moore (13)
Southam School

Demonic Vampires

D racula is their boss,
E vil lives they lead,
M aleficent they will always be,
O lder than they look,
N aughty things they do,
I mmortal features like a bat,
C rypts are where they like to stay.

V iper-like teeth will get you in a flash,
A stral places is where they like to fly,
M acabre they will always be,
P hantom, people think they are
I mpish creatures playing tricks.
R IP they never will,
E pitaphs will tell the story.
S ubterranean are their homes.

Sarah Brooks (13)
Southam School

Football

Football is a game
With eleven men and a ball
You dribble, tackle, shoot and score
But that's not nearly all.

'Goal' shouts everybody
Beckham heads it in
They run around the pitch
Desperately trying to win.

Gail Russell (12)
Southam School

SLEEPING ALONE

A cold, dark house, I'm all alone
The house, it's empty, there's no one home.

Slurping noises from the outside drain,
The crashing sound of rain on the windowpane.

The stiff creaks coming from the stairs,
The sort of things you'd only expect to happen
in the wildest of nightmares.

Sitting motionless, not moving a limb,
A crack of thunder, the lights go dim.

A look around the corner is all I dared,
Down the dark, gloomy corridor,
my horrified eyes stared.

At last I manage to fall asleep

. . . but the noises of that terrifying night,
forever I'll keep.

Amy McTaggart (13)
Southam School

VAMPIRES

V ampires are scary,
A nd very pale.
M ost get killed by a stake through the heart.
P eople don't like them,
I don't either.
R ight through the day,
E verybody is safe.

Wayne Clea (13)
Southam School

Vampires

Vampires love the dark,
Their fangs always leave a mark.
When daylight breaks,
Be ready with your wooden stakes.
Pierce it quick through the vampire's heart,
But it will leave a bloody mark.
Look at him with a face of white,
Be careful, he might just bite.
He will drink all your blood,
Believe me, he would if he could.
The vampire with his maleficent stare,
Pass him with the greatest care.
Be very aware on Hallowe'en night,
The vampire may give you a fright.
The epitaph on the headstone,
Remember this is the vampire's home.

Alex Biggerstaff (13)
Southam School

Maleficent Vampires

V ampires suck your blood
A ttacking whilst you sleep
M aleficent and macabre
P ale are their faces
I   nnocent their victims
R eturning to their subterranean grave
E pitaph covered in ectoplasm
S oul of a vampire is demonic.

Lisa Cooper (13)
Southam School

THE LAST VAMPIRE

In this subterranean crypt
A maleficent soul stirs in its sleep.
He must be aware as he maybe the last.
The mortals have learnt of things that warn us away
Or a stake through the heart, that to us do they slay.

The evil now stalks the astral night,
To find a lone victim to keep up his fight.
But then in the shadows a figure did appear
He has come to face the vampire without any fear.
He lunges and drives the stake through his heart
A banshee-like scream as the vampire shall depart.

The body now lies in a dark, dreary crypt,
The soul has departed,
But the vampire's not *dead!*

Jamie Maher (13)
Southam School

THE VAMPIRE THAT SUCKS

V ampires, blood-sucking creatures!
A bnormal people!
M acabre sort of feeling!
P ale grim little things!
I live my life in coffins!
R ecovering from a bite!
E ctoplasmic person!
S pectral kind of touch!

Rebecca McGovern (14)
Southam School

VAMPIRES RECRUIT

Rising as silently,
As a tiger upon his prey,
A soulless executioner,
Coming out to play.

Unsuspecting victim
Unconscious of the fact,
That an evil corpse,
Is about to attack.

In sink his teeth
The blood begins to flow,
Then as swiftly as he came,
He silently turns to go.

Following out of the window,
In quick pursuit,
The newly-drained victim,
Becomes his new recruit.

Becky Busby (14)
Southam School

VAMPIRE

V ampires striking in the night
A lways give you quite a fright.
M aking a mark when they bite
P ale skin.
I mpossible to escape
R unning away won't do any good.
E pitaph on the headstone.

Gemma Jackson (13)
Southam School

VAMPIRE

V ampire strolling through the night.
A lways looking to get you.
M aleficent a-fright,
P sychical eldritch.
I n the dark fearful and fright
R eal taste of blood.
E yes open wide, so keep them closed.

S ucks the tasty blood.
P hantom strolling into the dark.
I n the dark.
R eal taste of blood.
I n the dark.
T hen turns to look back.

Leaona Bourton (14)
Southam School

VAMPIRES

V ampires are very attracted to blood,
A nd a certain type of blood.
M oving hastily through the night,
    hunting their prey.
P eople are totally defenceless.
I n complete darkness,
R oaming our streets,
E nticing young women with promises of love
    then . . .
S ucking their blood, draining away their lives.

Natalie Waters (13)
Southam School

COBRA'S PREY

The snake slithers as slyly and as silently
as a cat burglar in a palace.

Its neck fans out ready to strike
a stroke of lightning to its victim
with venom like a lethal injection.

The snake stands tall and draws its victim in.
Its eyes light up ready to spill blood
on the bare desert sands.

The victim puts up a fight
but the cobra ignores it
and gives it a single vicious bite.

The victim falls to the ground with a loud shriek
and now the cobra can go and have a rest
and enjoy her feast.

William Bostock (12)
Southam School

VAMPIRES

V ampires, in the dead of night,
A lways ready to give you a fright.
M aleficent eyes watch your every move,
P repared for anything, as they can prove.
I gnore their hypnotic stare if you can,
R un, run like you've never before ran.
E very step he's closer, you feel him near,
S omewhere he's hiding, you're filled with fear.

Carol Hulme (13)
Southam School

Vampire

V ampire is looking for sweet blood.
A stral in the sky looking for the vampire.
M aleficent vampire walking around the street.
P erson hiding from the vampire.
I n freezing cold weather on a dark night.
R eflection, they don't like.
E ldritch vampire finding his person.

Katie Webb (13)
Southam School

Vampire

V ampires only go out at night,
A ll vampires are maleficent,
M r Dracula is the Count,
P ale faces, maleficent eyes,
I n the morning vampires sleep,
R eflections in mirrors they turn to dust,
E very night they look for victims.

Lisa Scott (13)
Southam School

Vampire

V ampires come out at the dead of night
A nd they give you an awful fright.
M aleficent comes to the brain
P eople crying in lots of pain.
I nto the victim they sink their teeth.
R eflections that do not come
E nd their night full of fun.

Dan Moreby (13)
Southam School

WITCH'S SPELL

Fifteen eyes and fifteen ears,
Lots of pies and a two fat deer.
Five slices of thick ham,
And a pot of ancient jam.

Ten loaves of mouldy bread,
And a bloke who looks half-dead.
Seventeen bogey-filled noses,
And a small bouquet of roses.

Seventy-five chocolate bars,
And a sky full of stars.
One awful computer game,
Also a dove which is tame.

A five sized leathery ball,
And a giraffe ten foot tall.
A twelve carat gold photo frame,
And the boiling cauldron flame.

Stephen Smith (14)
Southam School

VAMPIRES

V ampires roam in darkness.
A lways hunting for prey.
M aleficent is their soul.
P ale are their faces.
I n demonic dusty coffins they lay
there eyes to rest.
R eflections turn their bodies to stone.
E nding the bloodthirsty phantom.

Natalie Baillie (13)
Southam School

VAMPIRE

Vampires appear at night,
Astrals always in sight.

>Eldritch beings coming from the trees,
>A spirit looking at me.

Could this be a vampire?
With gorgoneion hairstyle, is
it a banshee, a dopplegänger,
I don't know? But it's scaring me

>As it gradually gets closer,
>My heart pounds 10 times faster,
>Gory beings staring at me,
>It's a vampire I can see.

What is happening,
I'm going really weak.
The blood is gushing,
All over my feet.

>The fusty carcass,
>Is now laid to rest.
>This horrible vampire is,
>Just like the best.

Reflections do not appeal to vampires,
They curl up and moan,
When they recover,
They turn to stone.

Simon Hughes (14)
Southam School

LIFE OF A POEM

Born on a Sunday
Shabby hospital bed

Home on a Monday
Leaky house instead.

School on a Tuesday
- ran away to hide.

Thrashed on a Wednesday
Felt much worse inside.

Court on a Thursday
New children's home.

Escaped on a Friday
'round the streets to roam.

Homeless on a Saturday
Feel so much alone.

Philippa Surgey (15)
Southam School

VAMPIRES

V   ampires drink blood,
A   strals always in the sky.
M   acabre and eldritch they are.
P   ale faced,
I   n the moonlight.
R   iding in the night,
E   nding at
S   unrise.

Adam Eastbury (14)
Southam School

The Vampire

Deep within the dark of night
A face of an unearthly white
Follows you through the swirling fog
You increase your speed to a jog.

You stop and turn around to see
You rest and wonder what's going to be
A figure creeps without a sound
She seems to float above the ground.

The wild green glow of angry eyes,
Are torches in the inky sky
Closer, closer they come still
And you begin to lose your will.

Out beneath the trees she comes
She licks her lips and utters 'Yum.'
Your legs feel like lumps of lead,
You fall, put your hands on your head.

You hear her breathing as she comes near
Your body is taken over by fear
You cry in pain, your neck is sore
After that you see no more.

Alex Elliott (14)
Southam School

A Summer's Morn

Little lambs being born,
On an early summer's morn.
Flowers blossom, green grass grows,
Babies walk round with warm bare toes.

People lying in the garden,
Children making dens.
People drinking ice-cold drinks,
Little girls with arms linked.

Kayleigh Myczko (12)
Southam School

WHO WANTS TO BE A BUS DRIVER

Oh dear what a fuss,
As they all crowd on the bus.

Round the corner, out the gates,
'Stop, stop we forgot Robert Thwaites.'

Back to school to pick him up,
Now to Longdon on up.

Past the shops, all the noise,
Wave to all the football boys.

Past the park and the bank,
Shouting, 'Stop,' was it Frank?

First stop here we are,
Is that Tom's red sports car?

Next stop Cherrie Bank,
Is that where I've got to drop off Frank?

Last stop of the day,
Now I've got to get my pay.

Wendy Dowdeswell (11)
Southam School

THE NIGHTMARE

Claw-like hands reaching out
grabbing at her hair.
Tearing, ripping at her skin
or any flesh that's bare.

As she runs thin trails of blood
go weeping on her skin.
Mixing in with tears of panic
which come gushing from within.

Panting quite like a sick dog
she waits for the sounds of morning.
But all she hears is the echo of her heart
coming back to her like a warning.

At last he comes from up above
as fast and swift as a dart.
As screams of terror burst from her lungs
he sucks the life from her heart.

Moving his blood-filled torso
he moves on into the night.
Leaving her body lying broken,
her skin turning deathly white.

Soon the first bird in the morning
awakes to sing its cheerful song.
The fear has truly vanished
but the scent of death will linger on.

Sophie Eadon (14)
Southam School

THE PET DOG

Long-coated hair,
With the colours white and brown,
Mixed together as if it was a painting,
His tail a sandstorm going flip-flap,
Breezing through the wind.

His size is like a massive bear,
Loyal, all stood up proud,
And now he's trapped,
Wanting attention, but instead just ignored,
He's caged and life is not worth living,
Then he lays all lonely, lazy and loyal,
Hoping a visitor will soon appear.

It speeds along with long hair dragging behind,
As he puffs and pants, after his next victim,
He struggles to keep up,
As his eyes start to bulge,
His tongue hangs out,
As he dribbles with anticipation,
And breathing becomes laboured,
He doesn't give up, and carries on with difficulty,
His prey scurries into the moonlight,
Leaving the dog, dying from hunger,
All confused and frustrated,
He wakes up, 'Woof! Woof"!
And is now no more a prisoner,
And runs free in the world,
Hoping he won't relive this nightmare.

Mark Anderson (12)
Southam School

SEAL

'Hello I'm Seal,' an amphibious mammal with flippers as limbs,
And I smile in the scorching sun,
I'm furry and cute and have big eyes,
Flip flap goes my tail as I swim away from danger.
The water snails after me,
I was as fast as lightning,
I could swim when I was first born,
But now I have a deadly virus,
And I'm dying, endangered and swimming slow,
My bark is loud but I cannot use it,
I'm lying on the ground, still, but crying,
I'm floating around, I look down,
I'm dead and lying on the ground.

Ginnene Taylor (12)
Southam School

THE CREATURE

While I walk through the whistling trees
When I walk upon the leaves
The crunching of the dead wood on the floor
With claw marks from its claws
It reaches out and grabs my hand
With one swipe of my blade the creature lies there dead
in the evergreen glade.
After years it rots away but after all the creature still lies
in the evergreen glade.
The trees sway in the moon's glaze but never forget the creature's
grave.
But it stirs and wakes from its death
You better turn back it might be too late.

Louise Owen (12)
Southam School

SPECTRAL VOID

Rain bombed the soil,
sending mud splashing in all directions.
The pale corpse seemed to attract the mud,
almost being swallowed by the greedy mouth of earth.

Sweat poured from every pore of the digger's body.
He drove the spade into the spongy soil,
as a clap of thunder rang through his ears.
He stooped over the lifeless corpse,
the vile smell hit him,
he withdrew his head in disgust.

A pool had formed in the makeshift grave,
the pool rippled as if disturbed by a lone phantom.

There was a chilling splashing as a body was silently rolled into;
the spectral void.
A chortle that executed the rain was loud and low.

David Mugleston (14)
Southam School

A WITCH

A witch is like . . .
A dried up old prune,
Her nose is like a mouldy carrot,
Her clothes are like snake's skin,
Her spells are like blood baths,
Her voice is like an earthquake,
Her manners are like a raging bull,
All things considered, a witch is a bit
like my sister!

Adam Robinson (12)
Southam School

Southam School

S illy teachers
O utstanding school
U gly people at school
T ime for lunch
H appy people at school
A funny uniform
M agic school.

S outham is the best
C oming to school is fun
H appy people at school
O utstanding pupils
O utstanding teachers
L uck when we go home.

Andrew Moore (11)
Southam School

The Caged Chameleon

The chameleon lies in his cage thinking he's alone,
but it's just a dream.
Slowly he awakes, opens his eyes and sees people
staring all around.
Like a predator would its prey.
So he closes his eyes and disappears from mans' eye
as he merges in with the scenery.
Hoping he's disappeared from the rest of the world.
But he's still on display, like an actor in a play.
Still in the same cold, cramped cage.
As he sleeps himself into an early grave.

Ceri Amphlett (12)
Southam School

MY KESTREL POEM

The king of the air
That follows with the wind.
The handsome bird
With the pointed wings.
It's like a bullet in the sky
It squawks when it sees it prey.
Sometimes cute,
Sometimes vision.
Brown and red at the same time.
Like velvet.
60cm wide, 6ins long.
Lives in valleys or on
Mountains sometimes.
Free as can be
But in a cage sometimes.
It's sad to see a bird
Like this in captivity.
You see them sometimes
On a drain-pipe.
It's a suitable perch
A feather on a twig
A kestrel is near about.
The female bird is larger than the male.
As it hovers.
The tail's a fan.
Isn't it amazing
How the head's so still?

Kirsty Anderson (12)
Southam School

Wandering Nights

As you wander through the night,
As you wander there's a fright,
As you wonder what lays behind,
The trees of blackness, that make you blind.

You've heard of the tale of the night,
You've seen the woods in daylight
You've heard of the killer,
You've heard of his prey.
You've heard of his thirst, for blood
. . . at the end of the day.

But still you wander, through the night.
You find the house out of moonlight,
The dark, black walls, darker than dark,
Large dark curtains hang like bark,
A large black door, tall and wide,
Kept away from Human eyes.

As you stand a cold wind blows,
And you shiver down to your bones.
Then you see the darkened figure,
Reaching out a red blood hand.

As it grips you on the shoulder,
You want to scream, but your lips are frozen
With a grip hard, not fine,
You want to run . . . run and hide.
Your feet are like lead; you cannot move.

As it bites with teeth of white,
Your scream echoes through the night,
But a panicked scream, will not be heard . . .
   as your body limply falls . . .
      now your life . . .
         is . . .
            no . . .
               more . . .

Angela Cox (14)
Southam School

THE BAT

In the cave he opens his eyes,
Wide and alert
To hear screeching all around.
He decides it is time to go
and see what is on the menu tonight.
As he emerges he sees bats swooping,
soaring, gliding like hang-gliders.
A body of razor-sharp teeth
through the midnight air.
Dodging owls and other hunters,
who come, snap! Like a trap.
In the thickness of the night
After eating their fill,
they skilfully yet carelessly swerve,
homeward bound.
Perhaps a little too carelessly
for snap! Like a trap, a hunter.
With a flurry and flapping of wings
a drop of blood is shed,
and another, and another
until the world of the bat is crimson.

Claire Haughton (12)
Southam School

DEAR GREAT AUNTIE FLOSS

My poor dead auntie,
deep down under the moist, dark ground.
Old and fragile, sitting alone without a sound,
Why oh why did she have to die?
Now up there high in the sky.
On her own for many a day.
Thinking back to the good old way.
Hardly able to speak with her old, chapped mouth.
So many smells smelt with her worn out nose.
Skin still soft like a folded rose.
The gleam in her deep blue eyes starting to fade.
On the table, a dinner for one, ready made.
Wrinkled like a used bed sheet.
Body as cold as the frosty sleet.
Lived through both world wars.
Cancer, heart attacks and diseases more.
Her hair like fluffy cotton wool.
An amazing life, now shabby and dull.
Now her feeble body dancing with joy.
Meeting her husband and her baby boy.
Up in heaven free from hate.
Back again with her soul-mate.

Anne-Marie Cosgriff (12)
Southam School

SCHOOL POEM

There was a boy at school
Who once fell off a stool
He had a lump on his head
And he covered it with bread
And now he looks such a fool.

Lee Jones (11)
Southam School

LEONARDO DI CAPRIO!

Born on Monday
Unaware of all my fame

Christened on Tuesday
Leonardo was my name

School of Wednesday
My talent shining through

Acting on Thursday
The theatres are brand-new

Films on Friday
I'm gathering some fans

Awards on Saturday
The speech is in my hands

Stardom on Sunday
The world is mine to claim.

Sally-Anne Southam (15)
Southam School

SCHOOL BUS

When the last bell rings
Of the day,
Everyone runs outside,
Round the corner,
Down the road,
To catch the last
School bus of the day.

Alice Telford (11)
Southam School

Autumn Mornings

It was a nice autumn morning
I could smell dew on the grass
I looked out of my window
Autumn's here at last.

I put on my coat
I ran down the stairs
I got out of my door
And autumn was there.

It looked cold on the hillside
The leaves were all crisp
You could smell the nice fresh air
And grey was the mist.

I went back inside
I got my dog off the lead
She scratched me with her claw
She got all excited
And pulled me to the door.

Crimson the leaves, brown and green
Red the apples all rosy and clean.
Autumn, autumn, no, no, no
Autumn, autumn, please don't go!

Lynsey Worrall (12)
Southam School

Phones

Phones commonly known as the *dog and bone*.
Ring, ring or a different tone
My sister's always on it
Nobody else allowed
Really annoying if you're in a crowd.

Lots of different sorts now
Mobile and hands free
Sorting out a phone a real shopping spree
Oh no, it's ringing again
It's driving us all insane
Nobody wants to answer it
Only my sister who can't live without it.

Alice Wright (12)
Southam School

TEACHERS

Teachers teach lots of subjects
Like English, art and RE
But my personal favourite of all these
Has got to be PE.

Teachers nag and groan a lot
All throughout the day
I wish they'd do it less often
That's all I have to say.

Teachers can be weird
They also can get mad
I don't see what's wrong with them
But they can't be all that bad.

Teachers can be cool
They also can be sad
I've got really nice teachers
So I'm very, very glad.

Charlie Hacker (11)
Southam School

SCHOOL

School is a place for learning,
On your first day your tummy's churning.

At times you'll be in trouble,
And sent to the head on the double.

At school you can have a laugh.
And after PE you'll need a bath.

But the teachers are really angels,
Or are they?

Danny Brookes (11)
Southam School

TEACHERS

S melly teachers
C ool teachers
H orrible teachers
O ld teachers
O dd teachers
L ots of teachers

Scott Simpson (12)
Southam School

SOUTHAM SCHOOL SPEED

Hustle and bustle to the tuck shop. People pushing in.
Then I get pushed to the back of the queue.
Then I decide that I will not get a chocolate bar
So I go outside. I run around playing games and shouting about.
I run inside and get my bag and run to my next lesson.

David James Camps (11)
Southam School

ALL THEY CARE ABOUT

I walked into my new class,
And everybody stared,
Was I a nice person?
Nobody cared.

The girls only cared,
About my hair, shoes and clothes,
The spots on my forehead,
And my big, ugly nose.

The boys only cared,
About my football,
Was I a goal scorer?
Or was I just a fool?

The teachers only cared,
Whether I was clever or not
Was I a genius?
Or was I just rot?

Dawn Rawlings (11)
Southam School

A DAY AT SCHOOL

When Monday comes it's school again,
Time to tax my tiny brain.
Breaks are best
I need the rest
Then after lunch it's back to work,
What a pain!

Jenna Mahoney (11)
Southam School

Southam School

Southam School is really cool,
it's next door to the swimming pool.
We go swimming every week,
I hope it doesn't spring a leak!
All the teachers are completely mad
but some of them are not too bad.
The uniform is very green,
it makes me feel like a runner bean!
In the library you must not talk,
around the school, always walk.
Up the maths block stairs I climb
I must not be late for tutor time.
This is the end, my poem is done,
Southam School is number one.

Vicky Milburn (11)
Southam School

A Winter's Day

The
wind is cold it
stings my face. The
sky is black the trees
are bare. Jack Frost is
freezing my fingers. The clouds
are as grey as a pencil
lead. My ears are red and my
nose is running. The snow is
up to my knees I am
most probably going to
freeze.

Hope Emily Jezzard (12)
Southam School

SCHOOL

School, school,
Southam's cool.
Reading, writing,
Always fighting.

Break time, lunchtime,
Home time's best.
But all the others,
Like the rest.

Teachers shouting
At each other.
'Don't do that,
I'll tell your mother.'

Girls are always
Being good
And boys are always
Throwing mud.

Got to go,
Teacher's coming.
I can almost
Hear him running.

All is silent,
Not a word.
The door swings open
In comes Miss.

Michael McTaggart (11)
Southam School

Southam High School

Southam High is a very nice school,
Some people are brainy and others are fools.

There are loads of lessons like English and art
But none is as fun as going down the park.

Every school is for us to learn
Jobs are for adults for them to earn.

But when it comes to having fun,
You'll be stuck doing homework, so there is none.

Michelle Wallwin (11)
Southam School

Another Species

Beyond the outer limits
In the world we know as space.
Solar systems just like ours,
May hold another race.
Living, breathing, walking creatures,
Maybe just like ours.
Some think they live on Venus;
Some think they live on Mars.
Maybe they do exist after all;
Maybe they don't exist at all.
Maybe it's true and we're not alone;
That this Universe holds other species unknown.
If it does and they've come down to Earth,
It'd be a hideous thought
If they were one of us.

Tom Blizzard (12)
Stratford High School

ON THE SEA

Gliding over waves on the sea,
About as softly as can be.
But don't blame me
If I'm sick,
Because this rubber tyre
Was the only tyre
I could pick!

Tomas Matthews (11)
Stratford High School

SCARED

S cared is when you tremble inside.
C autious of every side. Afraid of
A bang at the window. In
R eal panic of what might happen
E dgy of everything around you.
D eadly afraid of the wind howling hard.

Claire Davies (11)
Stratford High School

SUPPOSING

Supposing the sky turned a light shade of orange,
Whispering its way through the dreamy clouds,
The clouds force the intoxicating feverish orange to a halt,
Eating greedily everything in its narrow path,
There I saw a shimmering little green man,
'Who are you,' I said
I simply don't know . . .

Kimberley Powell (12)
Stratford High School

SUPPOSING

Supposing there are such things as UFOs
Do they come from Mars or Venus?
Who knows?

Supposing an alien had a bright green face,
Would it fit in with the human race?

Supposing they attacked us with their laser beams,
Or is that only among our dreams?

Supposing an alien went to our school
Would it be clever or would it be a fool?

Supposing . . . these things we shall never know
But beware should you ever see a vivid glow!

Jamie Southam (12)
Stratford High School

I LOVE

I love glimpsing the moon,
The lovely colours in the rainbow,
Rain dropping from the rooftops on to my head,
Birds singing and tweeting,
Rabbits running from field to field,
Squirrels eating nuts from trees,
Opening all my presents at Christmas time,
And the smell and taste of spaghetti bolognese
I love going downstairs at night
When it's dark
Falling asleep on the sofa
Waking up and eating chocolate
These are things I have loved.

Gemma Simpson (11)
Stratford High School

I Love

I love the look of a spider's web,
I love to run on the sand.
I love to watch the rising sun,
I love the smell of a hot cross bun.

I love to come home on a Friday night,
I love the taste of hot chocolate.
I love to wake up on a Sunday morning,
When the rest of my family is still snoring.

I love to sit down with a good long book,
I find it really relaxing.
I love special days of the year,
I love water when it's oh so clear.

I love, I love, I love.

Emily Podbielski (11)
Stratford High School

Supposing

Supposing another race,
There in outer space.
All the same things on Earth
And even the same birth.

I wonder what's really out there,
And do we really care?
Have they got the same body as us?
Should we really fuss.

Andrew Briffett (12)
Stratford High School

I Love...

I love treading on hot sand
on a hot summer day.
I love smelling the sea water and
drinking it out of the palm of my hand.
I love watching the mussel slowly
opening it's strong hard shell.
I love looking up at the seagulls flying
high into the sky.
I love finding crabs under the rocks
I love daring myself to touch the
Anemone no matter how they look.
I love watching the sun go down
and walking across the sand.

Sarah Arnold (11)
Stratford High School

Lady Macbeth

A user, manipulative and intimidating
Ruthless, a devilish creature
Scheming and ambitious
Evil, calculating and persuasive
Cold like a sheet of ice
Superstitious, emotional and egotistical
Thick blooded
Vicious like a prowling animal hunting
Slowly turning:
Insane
Broken
Suicidal.

James Fernandes (15)
Stratford High School

THESE I HAVE LOVED

Snow
Skin off custard
The smell of smoked bacon
Listening to music
Eating chocolate
Playing my keyboard
Freshly cut grass
Going into the sea
Taking my shoes and socks off and running
through hot sand in the summer
Running over hot tarmac when it is hot from the sun
Going on holiday
Going to bed
Watching the television
The smell of petrol
Having a good meal
Having a bath.

Mark Roberts (11)
Stratford High School

BEYOND

Beyond the beyond,
Above the unknown,
In adjacent atmospheres,
Intermingling with space,
Is there another race?
Walking and talking,
Gaping and gawking . . .
At us!

Alexander Barons (13)
Stratford High School

CREATURES OF THE NIGHT

Throughout the dark, eerie and peaceful night,
This red and satin fox can hunt his prey.
His blameless prey runs quickly out of sight,
One day, someday they say this fox will pay.

Throughout that same dark night the badgers play,
You must see their black and white bandit lines.
The badgers play, till at last they see day.
Their home tunnels are like the cold dark mines.

The big brown owl, sits in the big oak tree,
He watches closely and stately he sits.
He watches the fox and badger below
Before he too swoops to catch his prey.

But these creatures do hide when they see light
For these are only creatures of the night.

Lydia Burton
Stratford High School

SUPPOSING . . .

Supposing the door flung open and then,
Oh no it's the Martian visiting again!
I told him to go,
Do you think he listened? Oh no!
He was hairy and green!
That was the last I saw of him.
Off he went in his UFO,
Through the stars
And out to space,
And away from the human race.

Helen Goodman (12)
Stratford High School

Lady Macbeth

Obsessive, superstitious;
Infatuated, fixated;
Overpowering, devoted.

She is as menacing as the ominous hills of the highlands.

Calculating, scheming;
Ruthless, intimidating;
Persuasive, manipulative.

Her intentions are masked like fog masks the hills,
Hiding them until they draw closer, when the true colour becomes visible.

Hellish, satanic;
Deranged, possessed;
Insane, suicidal.

Amy Bishton (15)
Stratford High School

Our Cosmic Teacher

Supposing our teacher came from outer space
Strange and sinister
Come to destroy all the human race
Demolish and defeat
Took over the Earth
Commander and Chief
Bang!
Blast and burst
All but our alien teacher.

Zoë Gibbons (13)
Stratford High School

THE END OF THE EARTH

Supposing a UFO came down from space
Startle
Shock
It would mean the end of the human race
Catastrophe
Calamity
They might paint the world red
Magenta
Maroon
While everyone is lying dead
Perished
Paralysed
There are no more towers standing
High
Huge
More flying saucers landing
Disembark
Docking
No more human being
Humanity
Human kind
Little green Martians leaving
Microscopic
Miniature.

Stewart Crow (12)
Stratford High School

WILD

Wild is the engine that stutters and stalls,
Wild is the ivy that climbs the walls.
Wild are the calls the ravenous wolf makes,
Wild are the natives that hunt the snakes.

Wild are the punches boxers land,
Wild are the storms that whip over sand.
Wild are the steam trains that leave the station,
But wildest of all is our imagination.

Jack Wharton (12)
Stratford High School

DO YOU CARE?

Elephant tusks and
Tiger bones
Leopard skins and
Monkeys homes.

All being used for
Our greedy pleasure
Nobody cares
While we live in leisure.

Elephant tusks and
Tiger bones
Leopard skins and
Monkeys homes.

All being used for
One thing and another
But what of the animals
There are no others.

These animals are disappearing
Can't you see?
How would it feel
If it was you or me?

Nicole Wein (12)
Stratford High School

MY FANTASTIC GARDEN

My back garden grows and shrinks all year round.
Seasons come, and seasons go, wind, rain and snow.
The seasons change with a different sound
At the right time of year, sown seeds will grow
Our garden is swarmed with wasps every year.
Our barbecues and memorable nights
I can climb all our trees and have no fear
See fireworks reach incredible heights
The charred cinder of our bonfire remain
The top of our garden's an awful mess
The vegetable bush held up by a cane
The fruit they bear seems to get much less.
Yet my garden's such a brilliant place
I couldn't do without my garden's space.

Thomas Baker (13)
Stratford High School

UNTITLED

Ambitions, persuasive and overpowering
An emotional and obsessive woman,
Not naturally evil, but devious.
Her deeds return to haunt her
She becomes insane
A ruthless woman
With the unquenchable, raging ambition
Of an eternal fire.
The satanic wanderings of her mind,
Darkness has enveloped her soul.

Emma Jones (15)
Stratford High School

THE DRUMMIN' HUNK

As his white sheet slings to his hunky chest,
My eyes glare about his golden brown hair.
As he beats the sticks to try and do best.
The words of soft music call out Claire.
He stands with his hands in his jeans pockets
As the sound of Iaris name I overhear
Then I plug the keyboard into the socket
With a sudden clink everything came out clear.
As the chocolates are passed over to him
I cover my red face so he can't see
Then boys bug me acting like clever sins
Now I cry, for this will be the last meet
Will I ever see my love one more time?
Will he be one for the love of mine?

Melantha Thomson (13)
Stratford High School

LADY MACBETH

Glacial, stony sheet ice,
Encases the blistering froth of her ambition
Viciously ruthless,
Like a raging, red-hot fire.
Unearthly and dominant,
Imposing, a black castle
Towering over the Highlands
Unpredictable,
A passionate whirlwind,
Rampaging through Macbeth's doubting mind.

Jennie Needham (15)
Stratford High School

My Passion For Water

Heavens send down a large crash of thunder,
Then bolts of gold lightning, the storm begins,
Water falls from the sky filled with wonder
Thousands of drops descend, pricking like pins.

Caught and trapped the river takes them deep down,
Such a stunning view sets my heart on fire,
Whirlpools dancing beneath the liquid blue gowns,
Its sheer power longs for you to admire.

Follow its route, past its wicked outside,
Just to find a peaceful beauty below,
The cool waters waiting for me to ride,
I plummet the clear depths steady and slow.

We may take for granted this strange blessing,
But if without what would happen is no guessing . . .

Hannah York (13)
Stratford High School

Black-Hearted

Vicious and ruthless, a Scottish winter night;
A bottomless pit of evil -
Overpowering, a violent storm.
Raging ambition like a ruthless fire,
Consuming everything in its path.
Hard like granite rocks on the mountain,
A destructive gale,
Annihilating all around her.
She is a devil.

Anna Sanders (15)
Stratford High School

The Enchanted Flame

A flame that burns so strong before my eyes
Can be nothing but pure untouched beauty
Inside the flame a fierce power cries
To be let out, to run roaring and free.
A flame is like a daring ocean wave
They are both pure and they are both so calm
To these two things the world will have to cave
And neither will win battles using charm.
The wick on the candle slowly burns down
The flame's enchanted spell wearing it out
Once solid colour now is burnt out brown
But none can hear the wick's tortured shout.
The light grows dim and the flame flickers out
The enchanted flame we are now without.

Hannah Eastgate (13)
Stratford High School

These Have I Loved

I love listening to music.
I like the smell of chocolate.
I love watching lightning
And hearing thunder too.
I like to lie on a
Float in a swimming pool.
I love reading at night
Before I go to bed.
And most of all,
I love my bed so much!

Michelle De-la-Mare (11)
Stratford High School

COLOURS

Orange is bright and is a jazzy thing,
Red is hot and is the colour of hate,
Both these colours make me want to sing,
Yellow makes people want to celebrate.
Black is dull and makes people think of death,
Grass is green like the leaves on a spring tree,
White is the colour of autumn day breath,
Pink is the colour that makes you feel free.
Blue is the colour of the sky and sea,
Turquoise is bright and is very vibrant,
All different colours are special to me,
Grey is the colour of an elephant.
Silver is shiny but not the best yet,
Gold is the tops, like my Labrador pet!

Gemma Honor (13)
Stratford High School

THE WALK INTO WONDERLAND

Through the solar system,
Within the unknown,
Between planets,
Near outer limits,
Knock, knock, is anyone there?
Does anybody care?
Is there a world,
Beyond our world?
Are there villages?
Can we have pilgrimages,
To their planets?

Shelley Faulkner (12)
Stratford High School

My Friends

Let me tell you about my loyal friends:
Thomas Baker is fun and likes a laugh,
He's good at fixing and likes making mends.
On Christmas Day he sometimes has to carve.
Laura Cox is good at all sorts of things,
She likes to blade and grind and stuff like that.
She does not like flies and insects with wings,
But she's not afraid of things such as bats.
Carly Hanks used to like the unexplained,
She liked to watch programmes on UFOs.
But now Carly is well Internet trained,
She enters chat rooms to say her hellos.
My friends are different in their own ways,
They like to cheer about their own small craze.

David Rees (13)
Stratford High School

Bullet Point

- Footsteps are sounding
- Echo all around you
- Suddenly silence . . .
- Feel the breeze
- and the 'click' behind you
- 'Freeze . . .'
- A cold metal, pressing
- Heart, beating rapidly
- Chilling . . . bullet point.

Ben Whybrow (14)
Stratford High School

LADY MACBETH

Devilishly superstitious,
Evil and vicious.
The glacial stony sheet ice encases
The blistering froth of her ambition
Becomes devious, calculating and
scheming.
Ruthlessly manipulative,
Overpowering and persuasive.
Intimidating like the desolate moors
Surmounting the grim darkness
The oppressive fog of her cruelty masks
her weakness.
Insanely obsessive,
Suicidal, a broken woman.

Katie Shelton-Smith (15)
Stratford High School

THE UNKNOWN

Between the asteroids
Beyond the galaxy
Within the universe
Towards the solar system
Above the stars
Around the sky
Over the limits!
The misty moon
The bulbs of light
The colours shimmer
Another life form

Born now?

Hayley Ash (13)
Stratford High School

An Ocean

Ambitious, powerful, solid as an army
Blood of the devil engulfs her,
Swallows her, devours her.
Destructive as a hellish storm.
Emotional, passive as a chilling wind.
Weak, broken, unearthly grey,
Insane, suicidal, riding a rapid
Annihilation of the soul.

Lisa Griffiths (15)
Stratford High School

The Best Things In Life

The best things that I like in life are free,
My friends, *brother* and family.
Together we have a great laugh in life,
But we can still stay together through trouble and strife.

Joy Middleton (11)
Stratford High School

Lady Macbeth

A winter unpredictable, icy,
Glacial, stony sheet ice
Encasing the blistering froth of great ambition
Rancorous, ruthless like the severe biting wind,
The sinister fog obscuring a once amorous, maternal maid
Volatile, unstable, ready to explode.

Ella Selwood (16)
Stratford High School

PRISM

Look through a prism.
What can you see?
Can you see into the future,
Or do you see the past?

It is full of colours when light hits
Rainbow colour sparkle in the sun,
It turns round so colours are like a laser beam
When light goes the prism is dead.

Look carefully otherwise you miss what's happening,
Is it the right place to be?
A lot you have to ask yourself,
But you can never be sure of the answer.

Was your past good or was it bad?
Whatever it is you still had good things,
Look back on the old days,
Were they better than today?

Sally Hall (14)
Stratford High School

LADY MACBETH

Devious, calculating and vicious
Yet weak, emotional and insane
Cold
Enveloping as a freezing northern mist
Ruthless, deceitful and intimidating
Yet broken, suicidal and obsessed
Shattered
Destroyed by the evil she once invited into her.

Tom Fidler (15)
Stratford High School

THE SEASONS

Spring and the lambs on a dewy, wet day,
The sun breaking through the clear cloudless sky.
The bunnies and squirrels come out to play,
The horse on the hill with his tail held high.

Autumn is beautiful but yet so strange,
All colours ranging from maroon to gold.
The trees and the leaves, everything in change,
Silver and blue ice, reflecting the cold.

Wintertime is freezing and snow does fall,
An icy white sheet now covers the world.
Toboggan runs made, kids having a ball,
Hibernating animals, hedgehogs curled.

The rest of the seasons are cold and wet,
But summer is warm and is the best yet.

Claire Hawkins (13)
Stratford High School

THESE I HAVE LOVED

Running through a field of daisies
when the sun is setting.
The smell of hot cocoa at night
before you go to bed.
The smell of bacon sizzling in the morning
too hot to eat.
The path twisted all the way
makes me wonder,
will I last another day?

Anthony Green (11)
Stratford High School

WEALTH

Imagine
A fountain of all knowledge
The most detailed history book
    But with feelings
A lifetime's experience
    At your disposal
Do you know what I'm saying?

They drone
They mutter
They stutter
They groan
    But think
Are we really fair?
To these fountains of knowledge
These experienced citizens
    Of our community?
Now, do you realise what I'm saying?

Amy Wein (15)
Stratford High School

SUPPOSING . . .

Supposing there was a spacecraft outside the door,
It's just something I can't ignore.
What if there was a spacecraft outside the door?
One or two or maybe more.
Round and big and filling the street,
Something I wouldn't like to meet.
Little green men from outer space,
In their saucers all around the place.

Lucy Stanley (12)
Stratford High School

SUMMER

Summer's a time to relax and sunbathe,
Warm, sleepless, humid, restless summer nights,
Late nights partying at a summer rave,
Beware of nasty, stinging insect bites.

Go to the beach or sail on the ocean,
Slurping delicious vanilla ice-creams,
Better make sure you wear suntan lotion,
Let your skin soak up some tanning sunbeams.

Summer's the right time for T-shirts and shorts,
And messing about on that golden sand,
If you play pranks make sure you don't get caught,
If you're lucky enough you might get tanned.

The trouble is summer's not quite like that,
You'll often need a coat and a rain hat.

Hazel Ingram (13)
Stratford High School

BEYOND THE UNKNOWN

Beyond
Beyond the unknown
Something lies
That we don't know
Through the skies
Between the stars
Little green aliens
Go to Mars.

Alexandra Sophie Delin (13)
Stratford High School

A Sonnet About The Wonders Of The Sky

The sky is like a colour wash of paint,
The fresh day has a sky so bold and bright,
In the morning the strong blue seems so faint,
Silver stars shining from the deep, dark night.

The shimmering sun fades into the sky,
Glowing like a raging ball of fire.
Its rays beaming down on us from up high,
Up where there's everything you could desire.

The white, wispy clouds remind me of sheep!
Or pieces of soft, fluffy cotton wool,
It starts to rain, making puddles so deep,
The murky rain puddles make a big pool.

With the summer sun, clouds and rain and snow
There's many wonders of the sky, you know!

Sophie Parslow (13)
Stratford High School

Wonder Space

The universe
The unknown worlds
I want to see them!
The different galaxies
The similar atmosphere
Where is it?
What is it?
I don't really know . . .

Amanda Keech (12)
Stratford High School

LIFE

Life does begin and end in such strange ways,
You will begin your life so unaware,
You learn throughout the years, the months, the days.
So many things it can become a scare.

Life can be hard it makes you want to cry,
Or live at ease, no care at all in mind,
The stress, the strain, just give a little sigh,
Life's not easy, you might just have to find.

Many lovers but most just go astray,
With support from the people close to you,
But then you meet your man and he's OK,
You don't know why you love him but you do.

But then comes the end so sweet and so small,
And really your life seemed nothing at all!

Sophie Ellis (13)
Stratford High School

LOVE

My head aches from lack of sleep,
My thoughts are in a muddled heap.
Love prevents my head from rest
My heart is throbbing in my chest.
Everyone needs some affection to review their complexion
On their life and how it's been.
And if I could have foreseen,
Of all the wasted hours I've spent
Writing letters I never sent.

Lisa Leongamornlert (15)
Stratford High School

CHILD SCREAMS

The dark cloak slowly settles on the sky,
And everyone says that it is nigh.
The moon comes out to replace the light,
The stars come out twinkling brightly,
And everyone's just asleep, snoring slightly,
As a comet passes just in sight.
There is no sound,
Yet on the ground,
Small animals play in the dark,
Pretending they were on Noah's Ark.
But through the night there is a sound,
A monstrous animal falls on the ground.
The child awakes from his dreams,
And calls for mummy in his screams.

Selina Mayo (14)
Stratford High School

LITTLE GREEN MEN

Beyond the unknown
Way out in space
Around a corner
Lies a little green face
Down from the sky
Like a large fly
It releases a beam
As it goes to its extreme
They say goodbye
Or is it a lie?

Craig Hodgkins (12)
Stratford High School

BEYOND, BEYOND

Beyond, beyond the other world,
Over us all lies the crystal moon.
Near the galaxy,
Between the solar system,
Above the sky,
Through the stars,
No one knows,
But there is Mars!

Katie Wood (13)
Stratford High School

I WANT TO BE A POLICEMAN

I want to be a policeman
With a golden hat.
Going through the street
Like a royal cop.
Up, down, looking for criminals
Every day and night.

Adrian Mitchell (11)
Stratford High School

I LOVE?

I love the smell of chocolate and petrol.
I like watching TV with chocolate in my mouth.
I like the smell of new bags
And listening to music.
Opening new books and pencil cases.
I love the smell of flowers.
Sand in-between my toes when I am walking.

Holly Perry (11)
Stratford High School

These I Have Loved

Smelling the fresh doughnuts
Getting into bed and it's cold then it gets warm
When you're comfy
Tasting warm chocolate
The smell of bacon
Jacket potato for tea
Pop music
Popping poppers
Going into the sea and it's cold
Getting wrapped into a towel
Smell of petrol
Having a bath
Smelling a new exercise book
Putting your feet on a radiator.

Kevin Holt (11)
Stratford High School

The Classroom Window

I sit, watching, looking out of the window.
It's dull today.
Gloomy, late waking up as it's still a little dark.
The cold, fresh wind moves the tall delicate trees.
The autumn leaves are falling,
Red, orange, yellow and brown are the colours that smother the ground.
The mysterious hills in the mere distance are covered in mist.
Seagulls fly picking up yesterday's lunch.
A class waits, their teacher has not arrived.
They play,
Shouting, screaming with laughter,
Running around, burning off energy.
Tomorrow all this will be gone.

Siân Walters (14)
Stratford High School

ASTON VILLA

Who needs Dwight Yorke when we've got Paul Merson?
We have scored far more goals than ever before.
Gregory has certainly chosen the right person,
He has got talent we cannot ignore.
Gareth Southgate is a great defender,
Ready to prevent the opposing goals,
Getting the opponents to surrender,
As he scores our goals between the poles.
Mark Bosnich our Australian keeper,
He performs for us one hundred percent,
You can't get a better goalie, cheaper,
He keeps us shouting with great excitement.
Come on, you villains and please make us proud,
For your cheering and supporting crowd.

Sarah Hicks (13)
Stratford High School

ALONE

I was on my own with no protection,
All I had was my own reflection.
I had nowhere to go, no one to see,
But at least I knew that I was free,

I often thought about my life,
With all of the hassle and all of the strife.
Where was I going, what would I do?
If only I had someone too.

My life took a turn, one particular day,
I finally met someone who would stay.
We laughed and joked, I was happy again,
I knew I'd no longer feel the pain.

Elizabeth Blewer (14)
Stratford High School

CHOCOLATE

Chocolate is smooth and soft and creamy,
I eat it all day, I eat it all night,
And when I eat it I will feel all dreamy,
If I don't have some I will pinch a bite.
It's brown or white or even sometimes both,
I like dark chocolate, it's really nice,
I like them all but there's one more than most,
Make sure I hid it away from the mice.
Galaxy and Fuse Bars, Aeros and Mars,
I save all my money to buy some more,
Keep all my goodies locked up in a jar,
Chocolate, chocolate, I love it all.
Chocolate is lovely, and is the best,
When I melt it I will get in a mess!

Amiee Cotterill (13)
Stratford High School

THE SUN COMES OUT

Drip drop the rain falls down,
rapidly settling on the ground.
Snow falls in pretty snowflakes,
in all sorts of patterns snow can make.
The wind blows strong gales,
destroying the fisherman's sails.
Lightning and thunder crash and bang,
striking the bell as it rang.
The sun comes out shining bright,
clearing the dreadful thundery sight.

Rachael Coombes (14)
Stratford High School

HIGH AS A KITE

Flying in the blue sky would be my dream
As I fly I can see all kinds of things.
I fly to a branch and I lean
Then I wash my lovely long wings.
I see my friend, so I go to meet her
I saw a cat as happy as could be.
The cat was so happy that he would purr
As I'm a bird he would come and eat me!
I fly back to the tree to see the world
And I listen to the whistling wind go by.
I see a leaf go past me, it swirled
I then decided to go and have another long fly.
I see a fish pond and decide to eat,
As I fly down and I land on my feet.

Claire May (13)
Stratford High School

PARK BENCH

The icy chill of the wind,
Bites you like a shark.
The driving rain trickles down your forehead.
Gone now, the gentle bird song.
Gone now, leaves on the trees.
Bring on now the summertime,
Please . . . !

Tom Cox (14)
Stratford High School